BELIEVE
In God's
Miraculous
Power Today

Noah
- GOD Bless you
to Jaden!

An Inspiring
Devotional of
Scriptures &
Quotations

WH Federer

William & Susie Federer

BELIEVE IN GOD'S MIRACULOUS POWER TODAY
An Inspiring Devotional of Scriptures & Quotations
by William & Susie Federer

RELIGIOUS/SPIRITUALITY
paperback ISBN: 978-1-7369590-0-8

Cover design:
Dustin Myers, LongitudeDesign.com
(417) 986-2336 dustin@longitudebranding.com

Amerisearch, Inc., P.O. Box 60442, Fort Myers, FL 33906
1-888-USA-WORD
www.AmericanMinute.com, smfederer@gmail.com

Because we need to believe in the Almighty, Everlasting, Power of God ...

"We verily believe and trust the Lord is with us, unto whom and whose service we have given ourselves in many trials; and that he will graciously prosper our endeavors according to the simplicity of our hearts therin."

– Pilgrim Governor William Bradford,

Of Plymouth Plantation, 1630-1651

CONTENTS

SELECTED SCRIPTURES & QUOTATIONS

BELIEVE in God's Miraculous Power Today - William & Susie Federer

DEDICATION

This book is dedicated to inspiring you during these trying times. When it seems hopeless and you do not know what to do, pray and believe that God will move on your behalf. There have been many times in history when individuals prayed and God rescued them. We believe in Jesus for salvation — we must also believe in the power of His Name over all the obstacles in our life.

When it looks hopeless, we must keep our eyes on Jesus and remember His promises. When you have done all that you can do, pray and stand on the promises of God's Word.

Instead of letting the evil in the world overcome you with fear and depression, focus on the hope and promises of the Bible. It is our turn in history to be leaders and fight the good fight of faith.

I dedicate this book to our four children, their wonderful spouses, our beautiful grandchildren, our godsons and daughters, especially Bill's godson, Foster Thatcher Friess. I am believing for a bright future for each them, and a bright future for you who are reading this book!

Keep your Faith strong. May God's blessings be upon you!
— Susie Federer, 2023

❦

BELIEVE IN THE LAMB OF GOD

"The next day, John the Baptist saw Jesus coming toward him, and said, 'Behold! The Lamb of God who takes away the sin of the world!'" – John 1:29

♦

ON ACCIDENT OR ON PURPOSE

Did everything happen just by accident, or on purpose? Cambridge biochemist Rupert Sheldrake, author of *Morphic Resonance: The Nature of Formative Causation,* 2009, remarked in a TEDx Talk (Whitechapel, 1/12/13) "The Science Delusion":

> As (ethnobotanist) Terence McKenna used to say, "Modern science is based on the principle, 'Give us one free miracle and we'll explain the rest.'" And the one free miracle is the appearance of all the matter and energy in the universe, and all the laws that govern it, from nothing in a single instant.

It takes faith for an atheist to believe that, by chance, nothingness produced everything in an instant, that unguided random accidents created all things, from the unimaginably complicated DNA molecule to all that is beautiful, including selfless love, a baby's giggle, the masterpieces of Michelangelo, Da Vinci, Shakespeare, Beethoven, and the intelligence to appreciate them.

What about fractals? In mathematics, these are intricate geometric shapes made up of miniature renditions of that shape, made up of even smaller versions of the same shape, repeating in infinity.

Nobel Prize winning physicist Eugene Wigner wrote in "The Unreasonable Effectiveness of Mathematics in the Natural Sciences," 1960:

> It is difficult to avoid the impression that a miracle confronts us here ... or the two miracles of the existence of laws of nature and of the human mind's capacity to divine them.

If all things come from nothing, all things will eventually return to nothing, and your life is meaningless, just the result of millions of mindless mistakes.

Frank Turek and Norman Geisler published the book, *I Don't Have Enough Faith to be an Atheist* (2004), pointing out the irrationality of believing in nothing and the rationality of believing in a Creator.

Similarly, C.S. Lewis wrote in *The Oxford Socratic Club* (1944):

> If ... I swallow the scientific

cosmology as a whole, then not only can I not fit in Christianity, but I cannot even fit science.

If minds are wholly dependent on brains, and brains on biochemistry, and biochemistry (in the long run) on the meaningless flux of atoms, I cannot understand how the thought of those minds should have any more significance than the sound of the wind in the trees.

Oxford mathematician John C. Lennox said:

God to me ... is the explanation for the miracle of existence – why there is something rather than nothing ... The apostle Paul says what many pioneers of modern science believed, —that nature itself is part of the evidence for the existence of God ... Indeed, faith is a response to evidence ...

(That) clever mathematical laws all by themselves bring the universe and life into existence, is pure fiction. To call it science-fiction would besmirch the name of science ...

To the majority of those who have reflected deeply and written about the origin and nature of the universe, it has seemed that it points beyond itself to a source which is non-physical and of great intelligence and power.

Hebrews 11:3 states:

> Through faith we understand that
> the worlds were framed by the word of
> God, so that things which are seen were
> made of things which do not appear.

English poet William Cowper wrote:

> Nature is but a name for an
> effect, Whose cause is God.

Danish poet Hans Christian Andersen said:

> The whole world is a series of
> miracles, but we're so used to them we
> call them ordinary things.

♦

HOW CAN GOD GIVE US FREE WILL YET STILL BE IN CONTROL?

We believe God exists and is infinite in intelligence and power. He created all things, including us – beings made in His image with a free will. Though "all have sinned, and come short of the glory of God" (Romans 3:23), God had a plan of redemption. It is one thing to consider redemption from our point of view but imagine it from His. God is eternal—He has existed for eternity upon eternity. There never was a time when He did not exist.

> The High and Lofty One Who
> inhabits eternity. (Isaiah 57:15)

> I am the Alpha and the Omega,

says the Lord God, who is and was
and is to come. (Revelation 1:8)

He is omnipotent–all powerful; omnipresent–everywhere at all times; completely just; and immutable–perfect and unchanging.

For I am the LORD, I change
not. (Malachi 3:6)

God is omniscient–all knowing. "Lord, Thou knowest all things." (John 21:17) It is not so much that He knows everything – it is impossible for Him not to know everything. He created everything and continually holds everything in existence:

I am the LORD that maketh
all things. (Isaiah 44:24)

By the word of the LORD
were the heavens made; and all the
host of them by the breath of his
mouth. (Psalm 33:6)

Thou, even thou, art LORD
alone; thou hast made heaven, the
heaven of heavens, with all their
host, the earth, and all things that
are therein, the seas, and all that is
therein. (Nehemiah 9:6)

Genesis 1:3 states "And God said, Let there be light: and there was light." Light, as defined by physicists, is when an electron collides with its anti-matter opposite–a positron, resulting in them annihilating each other and creating two photons with no mass carrying quantum packets of energy traveling in oscillating perpendicular waves through the universal electromagnetic field at the speed of 186,282 miles per second.

Visible light (red, orange, yellow, green, blue, violet) is a small set of frequencies on the electromagnetic field spectrum. Light also includes non-visible waves: higher energy frequencies with shorter wavelengths, such as ultraviolet rays, x-rays, gamma rays, cosmic rays; and lower energy frequencies with longer wavelengths, such as infrared, microwaves, radar waves, and radio-broadcast waves, which can be rendered into sound and video.

In creating light, it necessitated God create the electromagnetic and gravitational fields that fill the universe, and, according to quantum field theory, a potential myriad of overlapping fields, whose vibrations result in the existence of subatomic particles of matter (called "fermions") and force-carrying particles (called "gluon bosons"), out of which are formed everything in existence.

According to Einstein's theory of relativity, $E=MC^2$, the closer one travels approaching the speed of light, the more time slows down. Theoretically, if someone could travel at the speed of light, they would experience time as if it were standing still.

Since God created light, He is obviously faster than light, so to Him every moment effectively stands still – a concept our minds will never comprehend. Yet, we get a glimpse of this in II Peter 3:8: "A day is with the Lord as a thousand years." Imagine experiencing a day as if it were a thousand years!

Since God created time, He is outside of time. He exists in the ever-present now–"I AM THAT I AM." For Him to create our reality, He had to make "space" where things move in "time." The speed limit He set for things to move in time is the speed of light in a vacuum. This is called the invariant speed of causality—the delay between cause and effect, keeping everything from happening at once.

Dr. Matt O'Dowd, in the PBS SpaceTime video "The Speed of Light is NOT about Light" (@pbsspacetime), explained that for the universe to exist, things have to move slower than infinity. This maximum cosmic finite speed limit is notated as "c.":

> "C" is the speed of light but it's the speed of causality first … It's the maximum speed at which any two parts of the universe can talk to each other … It's the only speed that any massless particle can travel … So light, or photons, also gravitational waves, and gluons, all have no mass, and so they travel at the maximum possible speed …
>
> So, what happens without a universal speed limit, and we pretend "c" equals infinity? There (would be)

no matter because it would take infinite energy to make any mass. There (would be) only massless particles traveling at infinite speed. Time dilation and length contraction (would be) infinite. There (would be) no time and space, no cause or effect, because all locations and times communicate with each other instantly. The universe (would be) an infinitesimal here and now.

This is all pretty paradoxical ... however the paradox itself tells us that an *infinite* speed limit is impossible. The *finite* speed of causality is fundamental to us having a universe in the first place.

In other words, God created light and set the speed of light—the delay between cause and effect—to keep everything from happening at once. In the infinite presence of the I AM THAT I AM everything is "now." God created the speed of light to be slower than "now," slower than infinity, a decelerated state. From God's point of view, we live in ultra-slow motion.

Time moves forward, not backwards. The smallest unit of time ever measured is a zeptosecond (a trillionth of a billionth of a second). Time is like a solar flare in a gravitational arc from the presence of God and back to the presence of God. We make our limited free will decisions in time, but since He is outside of time, He adjusts every electron in the universe before He has time move forward to the next nano-frame, ultimately arriving at "the day of eternity." (2Peter 3:18) God existing outside of time ensures His will takes place. He even arranged it so you would be reading this book right now!

Our limited free will exists only inside the context of His unlimited sovereign will.

♦

UNIVERSE DISPLAYS GOD'S INFINITE POWER

To get a perspective into how all powerful God is, consider the immensity of the universe.

In 1990, the Hubble Space Telescope was launched into low Earth orbit. In 2003–2004, the telescope was focused on a tiny spot in the sky where there was nothing – the Hubble Ultra Deep Space Field. This spot was tiny, the size of a grain of sand held between your fingers at arm's length against the night sky.

After a total of 11 days, the telescope images were examined. To the amazement of astronomers, in that little spot, where there was thought to be nothing, were ten thousand galaxies with hundreds of billions of stars in each galaxy. The photo revolutionized astronomers' understanding of the universe.

There was something else. As mentioned earlier, light travels in waves. On one end of the electromagnetic spectrum is the shorter, faster, high energy blue wave, and on the other end is the longer, slower, low energy red wave. Distant galaxies displayed a "red shift," indicating they are moving away from the Earth.

If galaxies are moving away from us, then in the past they would have been nearer. The Big Bang Theory is that at some distant time in the past, everything originated from one infinitesimally small spot till some infinitely powerful force propelled it away.

Prior to the 20th century, scientists predominantly thought the universe was unchanging, consisting mainly of our Milky Way galaxy. This changed in 1924 when astronomer Edwin Hubble observed the Andromeda Galaxy, the next nearest galaxy.

At Mount Wilson Observatory in Pasadena, California, using the world's largest aperture telescope of its day, with a 100-inch lens, Hubble confirmed that Andromeda was not a nebula – an interstellar cloud – but rather an entirely separate galaxy containing a trillion stars approximately 2.5 million light-years from Earth.

In 1931, Hubble invited Albert Einstein to look through the telescope. Einstein considered the "red shift" of distant galaxies as evidence the universe was expanding and remarked: "I now see the necessity of a beginning."

The unimaginable distances galaxies are from Earth are calculated by comparing varying intensities of stellar light, fluctuations in cosmic microwave background, baryon acoustic oscillations, and parallax observations — the process of observing an object in the sky from different points in the Earth's orbit around the Sun, similar to looking at a near object through your right eye and then your left in relation to the backdrop of distant objects and calculating the different angles.

The distant galaxies observed in the Hubble Ultra Deep Space Field are over 47 billion light-years away. Astronomers now estimate that the observable universe is 93 billion light-years across — and still expanding at the speed of light!

The James Webb Space Telescope, 100 times more powerful than Hubble, was launched December 25, 2021. Webb's First Deep Field revealed more distant galaxies in astounding detail.

There are estimated to be 10 trillion galaxies in the universe, containing over 2 trillion trillion stars. Between them is theorized to be ever expanding dark matter and dark energy, detected indirectly by gravitational forces.

The largest star found so far is Stephenson 2-18. It is a super gas giant, so large that if you were to place it in our solar system it would engulf the orbit of Saturn, the 6th planet from the Sun. The Earth is the 3rd planet. Can you imagine one single star being that enormous? And God made it all — the entire universe:

> Thus saith the Lord ... I, even my hands, have stretched out the heavens. (Isaiah 45:12)

> The LORD, he that created the heavens, and

stretched them out. (Isaiah 42:5)

Who stretchest out the heavens like a curtain. (Psalm 104:2)

The LORD thy maker, that hath stretched forth the heavens. (Isaiah 51:13)

God ... which alone spreadeth out the heavens. (Job 9:2-8)

The next time you pray "Our Father, which art in heaven," remember that you are praying to the infinite God who created and holds in existence the entire universe. You can trust Him with the situations you face in your life.

♦

SUBATOMIC PARTICLES DISPLAY GOD'S INFINITE POWER

The authors of this book admit they are neither scientists or theologians, nevertheless every new scientific discovery seems to confirm the vastness of God's creation, from the immensity of the universe to the subatomic particles that make up everything.

The largest measurement is the entire observable universe, measured at 10^{27} meters across. The smallest measurement, called a planck, is the width of two light waves converging at 10^{-35} meters. We basically live in the middle between the largest and smallest measurements.

Our bodies are made up of cells, each measuring about 10^{-5} meters in size. Cells are made up of organelles, which are made up of proteins, which are made up of amino acids, which are made up of molecules, which are made up of atoms, each having a nucleus made up of positively-charged protons, and neutrons with no charge, surrounded by negatively charged electrons which are 1,800 times smaller than a proton, being visualized to be spinning in a 720 degree angular momentum.

Atomic particles have mass, velocity, momentum, and energy. This all sounds innocent enough, but when certain atoms are split apart it can cause a chain reaction nuclear explosion powerful enough to flatten a city.

The science of particle physics, called "quantum mechanics," has led to experiments at the CERN Hadron Particle Collider, a 17-mile circle 574 feet underground near Geneva, Switzerland. When photons collide, they can create "matter," namely, negatively charged electrons, and "anti-matter," oppositely charged positrons. Imagine that, light creating matter!

Other experiments accelerate particles using super conducting magnets and smash them into each other, splitting them into tinier fermion particles called "quarks," which exist only for milliseconds before disappearing. A proton is made up of two up quarks and one down quark; and a neutron is made up of two down quarks and one up quark.

Quarks are classified in six flavors: up,

down, charm, strange, top, and bottom, and exhibit properties of mass, electric charge, color charge, and spin, and are held together by "gluon boson" exchange particles.

For every quark there is an anti-quark of opposite charge. Some neutral particles are their own anti-particles, namely, mesons, gravitons and some hypothetical WIMPs.

If you are not yet confused, there are even more subatomic classifications, such as: hadrons, higgs, ions, pions, baryons, leptons, muons, taus, nearly massless neutrinos, called ghost particles, 6 million times lighter than an electron, and "virtual" particles.

Amazingly, the smallest particles appear to have no mass and display a wave–particle duality with properties of both matter and energy.

Energy exists as a charge in an electric field. Charges in motion create a magnetic field. Electromagnetic energy is emitted or absorbed between particles through photons. These particles move so incredibly fast that at any one point in time it is impossible to know exactly where they are. This is called "the uncertainty principle," with the smallest particles theorized to be constantly coming into and going out of existence.

Quantum Field Theory proposes that these subatomic particles may actually be made up of waves of very defined, specific quantum frequencies.

The Bible speaks of God creating "the highest part of the dust of the world":

> While as yet He had not made the earth, nor the fields, nor the highest part of the dust of the world. When he prepared the heavens, I was there. (Proverbs 8:26-27)

G.K. Chesterton wrote in *The Everlasting Man*, 1925:

> Nobody can imagine how nothing could turn into something. Nobody can get an inch nearer to it by explaining how something could turn into something else.

> It is really far more logical to start by saying "In the beginning God created heaven and earth" even if you only mean "In the beginning some unthinkable power began some unthinkable process."

> For God is by its nature a name of mystery, and nobody ever supposed that man could imagine how a world was created any more than he could create one.

Eric Metaxas wrote in "Science Increasingly Makes the Case for God" (3/25/15):

> Today there are more than 200 known parameters necessary for a planet to support life—every single one of which must be perfectly met, or the whole thing falls apart … The odds

against life in the universe are simply astonishing. Yet here we are, not only existing, but talking about existing. What can account for it? Can every one of those many parameters be perfect by accident? At what point is it fair to admit that science suggests that we cannot be the result of random forces?

Doesn't assuming that an intelligence created these perfect conditions require far less faith than believing that a life-sustaining Earth just happened to beat the inconceivable odds to come into being?

There's more. The fine-tuning necessary for life to exist on a planet is nothing compared with the fine-tuning required for the universe to exist at all …

The greatest miracle of all time, without any close seconds, is the universe. It is the miracle of all miracles, one that ineluctably points with the combined brightness of every star to something—or Someone—beyond itself.

God not only created everything, He continually holds everything in existence

In the beginning was the Word,
and the Word was with God, and the

Word was God ... All things were made through Him, and without Him nothing was made that was made. (John 1:1-3)

Hebrews 1:1-3 (NIV) states:

God ... in these last days he has spoken to us by his Son, whom he appointed heir of all things, and through whom also he made the universe. The Son is the radiance of God's glory and the exact representation of his being, SUSTAINING ALL THINGS by his powerful word.

Colossians 1:13-17 states:

Christ is the visible image of the invisible God. He existed before anything was created and is supreme over all creation, for through him God created everything in the heavenly realms and on earth. He made the things we can see and the things we cannot see ... Everything was created through him and for him. He existed before anything else, and HE HOLDS ALL CREATION TOGETHER.

The Amplified Bible worded it:

He Himself existed and is before all things, and IN HIM ALL THINGS HOLD TOGETHER. [His

is the controlling, cohesive force of
the universe.]

The size of things does not matter to
God. He created, controls and holds all things
in existence – from the infinitesimally small
subatomic particles to the limitless, ever-
expanding universe. And He created your spirit:

> The LORD, which stretcheth forth
> the heavens, and layeth the foundation
> of the earth, and formeth the spirit of
> man within him. (Zechariah 12:1)

♦

WHY DID GOD MAKE US?

Face it. God is unfathomably awesome,
infinitely intelligent, and incomprehensibly
powerful, creating and holding all things in
existence—time, matter, space and energy.

Why would He make us? What could you
possibly offer this Being? Job asked "Can a
man be profitable unto God?" (Job 2:22)

But there is something you could offer
Him — your love, given of your free will!

Inside the framework of everything He
sovereignly controls, He intentionally created
one tiny thing He does not control – your will.
Now, He could control it if He wanted to, but
that would defeat the very reason He made us
different than everything else.

Think of how complicated you are. It took
unsurpassed creative power and intelligence
for God to make matter out of nothing, then

assemble it into a living organism, then form it into you—a thinking, reasoning human being made in the image of God, with the capacity to love Him as an act of your free will.

What is a galaxy anyway? It is a bunch of rocks: hot rocks, cold rocks, enormous rocks, molten rocks, vaporous rocks. A rock cannot love you. It is almost as if God said—been there, done that—I can make enormous things that obey me and subatomic things that obey me. I would really like someone in my image that could love me!

Other than mankind, all other creatures act as God created them to act. If they were to show Him affection it would be because He programmed it into them, so in reality it could not really be classified as love.

What about angels? Angels are mentioned 289 times in the King James Bible. Never once does it say the angels love God. The word "angel" means "messenger." They deliver God's messages, dispense His judgments, and defend His chosen people as "ministering spirits, sent forth to minister for them who shall be heirs of salvation." (Heb. 1:14) They give understanding, testify of God, and are heavenly witnesses who "sang together and ... shouted for joy" when God created the heavens and the earth. (Job 38:7) They are "fellowservants" who rejoice "over one sinner that repenteth." (Luke 13:15) They stand in God's presence, praise Him, and glorify Him.

But angels are not made in God's image and Jesus did not die on the cross to redeem angels. Angels cannot forgive, they just obey. The word "love" is not used in any verse in the Bible to describe an angel's relationship with God.

Angels have a free will, but it is in the constant awareness that there can only be one will in Heaven – God's. The moment there are two wills there is division, conflict, —war in heaven. The Greek name for devil is "diabolos" which can be translated "to divide." Angels know if they choose their will over God's, they will be instantly cast out of His presence like lightening with no chance of forgiveness or redemption. A king has a castle with mighty and intelligent staff, but then the king also has children. Angels are mighty and intelligent beings created for a purpose.

What purpose were you and I made for? We are not very smart and not very powerful. There is one thing we can do that angels cannot—we can love God! The word "love" is used all throughout the Bible to describe men and women's relationship with God.

> Love the LORD your God with all your heart, with all your soul, with all your mind, and with all your strength. (Mark 12:28-34)

> O love the LORD, all ye his saints. (Psalm 31:23)

> Because he hath set his love

upon me, therefore will I deliver him. (Psalm 91:14)

After rising from the dead, Jesus asked:

Simon Peter ... son of Jonas, lovest thou me? (John 21:15-17)

Billy Graham described the purpose for which God created us:

God created us for one reason: to know Him and love Him and have fellowship with Him. Adam and Eve loved God and had unbroken fellowship with Him. They not only lived in a perfect world, but they had perfect fellowship with their Creator.

But God created them with a free will—that is, with the ability to either love Him or reject Him. Otherwise, they would have been like robots, unable to choose to love God.

We may enjoy watching a robot in action—but we can't really love it, nor can it love us. And that's why God didn't make us like robots.

Instead, He gave our original parents the ability to love Him—or even reject Him. True love requires the ability to respond.

We may sin by choosing our own will, but we can repent. We can know God through His redeeming love, something angels will never know. And God *wants* us to know Him.

> But let him that glorieth glory in this, that he understandeth and knoweth Me. (Jeremiah 9:24)

Thomas Aquinas wrote in *Summa Contra Gentiles,* 1269-1265:

> To know God by an act of understanding is the ultimate end of every intellectual substance.

Harvard's Rules & Precepts, 1642, stated:

> Let every student be plainly instructed, and earnestly pressed to consider well, the main end of his life and studies is, to know God and Jesus Christ which is eternal life, John 17:3.

St. Augustine wrote:

> Oh, God, to know you is life ... To praise you is the soul's joy and delight.

The Westminster Shorter Catechism, 1647, explained:

> Man's chief end is to glorify God, and to enjoy Him forever.

Sir William Blackstone explained in *Commentaries on the Laws of England,* 1765-1769, that God made man different than all the rest of creation—with reason and free will:

> When the Supreme Being formed the universe, and created matter out of nothing, He impressed

certain principles upon that matter, from which it can never depart, and without which it would cease to be ...

When He put the matter into motion, He established certain laws of motion, to which all movable bodies must conform ... The greatest operations to the smallest ... from mere inactive matter to vegetable and animal life ... are not left to chance, or the will of the creature itself, but are performed in a wondrous involuntary manner, and guided by unerring rules laid down by the great Creator.

Man, the noblest of all sublunary (earthly) beings, (is) a creature endowed with both REASON and FREE WILL.

Astrophysicist Dr. Hugh Ross said at Mosaic Christian Church, January 30, 2020:

The creation texts in the Bible— what they all have in common is that they link the doctrine of creation with the doctrine of redemption ...

God begins His works of redemption before He creates anything at all, implying that everything God creates is for the purpose of delivering free will

human beings from their propensity
to commit sin and evil.

♦

LOVE CANNOT BE FORCED

God displayed His infinite creative ability
by bringing into existence us — beings in His
image whom He could love and who could
have the ability to freely love Him back. But
love, by definition, must be voluntary.

Love is a mysterious thing. The moment it
is forced, it evaporates. To compel someone to
respond may be obedience or submission, but
it is not love. If God were to force you to love
Him in the slightest way, He Himself would
know that He is forcing you and He would
know your response is not voluntary, not love.

If a guy intimidates, manipulates or twists
a girl's arm, and says, "tell me you love me," no
matter what she says she does not love him. But
if he provides for her, protects her, defends her,
rescues her, honors her, courts her, woos her,
cares for her, takes her out to a fancy dinner
and gives her flowers and chocolates, and out
of the abundance of her heart it bubbles up, "I
love you," then it means something!

This is what God is after. He is not
interested in – *submit or I will chop your head
off.* If He wanted that He could have forced
Adam and Eve not to eat from the tree, and
Jesus could have called down twelve legions
of angels to make people accept Him.

God will not force us to turn to Him, but

He does have Plan A and Plan B.

Plan A is — "The Lord make His face shine upon you" (Numbers 6:25) and blesses you so much you turn to Him out of gratefulness.

If that does not work, there is Plan B — "I will hide My face from them, I will see what their end will be" (Deut. 32:20; Isaiah 59:2; Job 13:24; 34:29; Psalm 44:24; 88:14; 104:29).

He lets us experience the consequences of our selfish decisions, then we turn to Him out of desperation. C.S. Lewis worded it this way:

> There are two kinds of people: those who say to God, "Thy will be done," and those to whom God says, "All right, then, have it your way."

Slave trader turned abolitionist John Newton, who wrote "Amazing Grace, said:

> It is a pity it should be so; but experience testifies, that a long course of ease and prosperity, without painful changes—has an unhappy tendency to make us cold and formal in our secret worship. But troubles rouse our spirits, and constrain us to call upon the Lord in good earnest ... Afflictions quicken us to prayer.

Oxford historian Arnold Joseph Toynbee wrote a 12-volume *Study of History* (1934-1961) in which he described the rise, flowering, and decline of 26 major cultures, from Egypt, Greece and Rome to Polynesia and Peru.

On March 30, 1956, as recorded in *Collier's Magazine*, Toynbee stated:

Civilizations die from suicide, not by murder ... When I started, religion was not a prominent feature ... In writing my study, I have been constantly surprised to find religion coming back to fill an even greater place.

So, what does the universe look like? ... It looks as if everything were on the move either toward its Creator or away from Him ...

The course of human history consists of a series of encounters between individual human beings and God in which each man or woman or child, in turn, is challenged by God to make his free choice between doing God's will and refusing to do it.

When Man refuses, he is free to make his refusal and to take the consequences.

When Man accepts, his reward for willing what is the will of God is that he finds himself taken by God into a partnership in the doing of God's creative work. When Man is thus cooperating with God, Man's freedom is at its maximum, because Man is then realizing the potentialities for which

God has created him. God has created Man to be God's free partner in the work of creation.

C.S. Lewis said in *Mere Christianity*, 1952:

All that we call human history—money, poverty, ambition, war, prostitution, classes, empires, slavery—is the long terrible story of man trying to find something other than God which will make him happy.

Lewis wrote in *The Problem of Pain*, 1940:

The human spirit will not even begin to try to surrender self-will as long as all seems to be well with it. Now error and sin both have this property, that the deeper they are the less their victim suspects their existence; they are masked evil. Pain is unmasked, unmistakable evil; every man knows that something is wrong when he is being hurt ...

God whispers to us in our pleasures, speaks in our conscience, but shouts in our pains: it is His megaphone to rouse a deaf world ...

No doubt pain as God's megaphone is a terrible instrument; it may lead to final and unrepented rebellion. But it gives the only opportunity the bad man can have for amendment; it removes

the veil; it plants the flag of truth within
the fortress of the rebel soul ...

Suffering is not good in itself.
What is good in any painful experience
is, for the sufferer, his submission to
the will of God ... If tribulation is a
necessary element in redemption, we
must anticipate that it will never cease
till God sees the world to be either
redeemed or no further redeemable.

When things get bad enough, we turn to
Him in our brokenness, and He rescues us.

II Chronicles 7:14 "If My people who are
called by My name humble themselves and
pray and seek My face and turn from their
wicked ways, then I will hear from heaven,
forgive their sin, and heal their land."

Jeremiah 15:19 "This is how the LORD
responds: 'If you return to me, I will restore you.'"

His big picture goal is for us to freely
turn to Him, as He does not want us to spend
eternity away from Him.

The Lord ... is long-suffering
to us-ward, not willing that any
should perish, but that all should
come to repentance. (II Peter 3:9)

♦

GOD GIVES YOU GRACE TO RESPOND
Your credit card has a tiny computer chip
in it, but no battery. It has no ability to conduct

a transaction on its own. It can only respond. When you go through a checkout line, an electronic signal from the bank travels to the store, to the cash register, to the chip reader, to your card's chip.

If the chip is working right, it bounces the signal back and your transaction is completed. All the chip has to do is respond to the energy sent to it. But if the chip is scratched, bent, or somehow insensitive, no transaction takes place.

Your heart is like that chip. You have no battery power to save yourself. But when you hear the Gospel message — that through the sacrifice of Jesus you are forgiven — that message has within it the spiritual energy, the grace, to enable you to respond. You simply surrender to it, yield to it, cooperate with it, participate with it, believe it. God sends His love to your heart, all you have to do is accept His love by faith and respond by loving Him back.

Don't let your heart be hardened or stiff-necked, for if you refuse to respond to God's love and grace, no transaction takes place.

Today, if you hear His voice, harden not your hearts. (Psalm 95:7; Hebrews 3:15)

Whoever hardens their heart falls into trouble. (Proverbs 28:14)

They hearkened not unto me ... but hardened their neck. (Jeremiah 7:25; 17:23)

Every love relationship first begins with

one person risking rejection to initiate it. The other person then has the choice of responding.

> We love him, because he first loved us. (1John 4:19)

> The goodness of God brings men to repentance. (Romans 2:4)

> No one can come to Me unless the Father who sent Me draws him. (John 6:44)

> But God demonstrates His own love toward us, in that while we were still sinners, Christ died for us. (Romans 5:8)

♦

GOD DOES NOT NEED YOUR LOVE BUT HE WANTS IT

God does not "need" your love. He is not incomplete in any way and your love somehow completes Him. No. He is complete all by Himself. He does not need your love, but He wants it! Just like parents do not "need" the love of their children, but they want it.

> Jesus saith unto him ... Simon, son of Jonas, lovest thou me? (John 21:17)

Though Adam's sin resulted in all of us being born with a fallen nature, yet even in our fallen state, there are still things we can deduce about God's nature by looking at how He made us in His image. Jesus explained:

> If ye then, being evil, know how to give good gifts unto your children,

how much more shall your Father
which is in heaven give good things
to them that ask him? (Matthew 7:11)

So, let's look at how He created us —
what is the most important thing in your life?
Is it material possessions, travel, recreation,
career, or prestige? I would venture to say that
somewhere at the top of your list, whether
you acknowledge it or not, are matters of the
heart. The universal cry deep within every
human soul is to love and be loved, regardless
of whether that person is a woman, man, girl,
boy, black, yellow, red or white.

If we are all made in God's image, would
it not then follow that maybe loving and being
loved is important to God? The Bible says,
"God is love"; "For God so loved the world
He gave His only begotten Son"; "The word
of the LORD to Israel through Malachi, 'I
have loved you.'"

There is something about love – the more
you love someone, the more you want that
someone to love you back. You are precious to
God, and He loves you infinitely, and He has
an infinite desire for you to love Him back.
It is the primary reason He created you. Yet
He will never force you.

God has already existed forever and
forever. He could have spent an entire eon of
that eternity just designing you!

Before time existed, He imagined a
wonderful, unique plan for your life, which

includes loving Him. "This grace was given us in Christ Jesus before the beginning of time" (2 Timothy 1:9); "In the hope of eternal life, which God, who does not lie, promised before the beginning of time." (Titus 1:2)

And since God is everywhere at the exact same time, that means He is presently, immediately and intimately in your face every moment, seeking your attention, wanting a relationship with you.

> True worshipers will worship the Father in spirit and truth; for the Father *is seeking* such to worship Him. (John 4:13)

> The Lord is near to all who call upon Him. (Psalm 145:18)

> The Lord is nigh unto them that are of a broken heart. (Psalm 34:18)

> He is not far from each one of us. (Acts 17:27)

> You are near, O Lord (Psalm 119:151)

God wants a friendship with you:

> Abraham believed God, and it was accounted to him for righteousness. And he was called the friend of God. (James 2:23)

> Abraham My friend. (Isaiah 41:8)

> Henceforth I call you not servants ... but I have called you friends. (John 15:15)

God is a spirit. We can love Him directly through prayer, praise and worship, and indirectly by showing our love to others, each of whom are made in His image.

> Whatever you did for one of the least of these brothers and sisters of mine, you did for me. (Matthew 25:40)

> Peter ... said unto him, "Lord ... Thou knowest that I love thee." Jesus saith unto him, "Feed my sheep." (John 21:17)

If you are a single person longing for someone to love you – or a married person longing for an estranged spouse – that is, in a sense, how God feels towards you. You are set apart for Him, the "ekklesia," the church, the "bride of Christ." His banner over you is love. (Song of Solomon 2:4)

In every love story, there comes that moment where a decision needs to be made – a forsaking of all others and choosing the one. How else does one show how much they love a person other than by what they are willing to give up for them.

Jesus gave up everything for you — "Greater love hath no man than this, that a man lay down his life for his friends." (John 15:13) "For you were bought at a price." (I Corinthians 6:20) At some time in your life, that moment will come when you can make your decision to give up everything for Him.

In the Old Testament, the Lord is referred to as "husband" married to His "bride" Israel. (Song of Songs, Isaiah, Jeremiah, Ezekiel,

Hosea) In the New Testament, John the Baptist proclaimed of Jesus "He that hath the bride is the bridegroom." (John 3:29) Jesus referred to Himself as "the Bridegroom." (Mark 2:19) Paul wrote that believers are the bride:

> For I have betrothed you to one husband, that I may present you as a chaste virgin to Christ. (2 Corinthians 11:2)

> Husbands, love your wives, just as Christ also loved the church and gave Himself up for her. (Ephesians 5:25-27)

John wrote in the Book of Revelations:

> There came unto me one of the seven angels ... saying, Come hither, I will shew thee the bride, the Lamb's wife. (21:9)

> I, John, saw the holy city, New Jerusalem, coming down out of heaven from God, prepared as a bride adorned for her husband. (21:2)

> The Spirit and the bride say come ... Even so, come Lord Jesus. (21:12, 17)

Most husbands get jealous if their bride is spending more time thinking about someone else. It is awesome to ponder that the God who created the universe loves you so much He is actually jealous for you to think about Him. He does not *need* it, but desires your attention, your affection. "For the LORD, whose name is Jealous, is a jealous God." (Exodus 34:14)

♦

WHY DOESN'T GOD JUST SHOW HIMSELF?

God created us as free will beings with the unique ability to love Him, but He also had to create the conditions – the OPPORTUNITY. For this reason, He had to hide Himself behind His creation.

> Verily thou art a God that hidest thyself. (Isaiah 43:15)

> I cannot behold him: he hideth himself on the right hand, that I cannot see him. (Job 23:9)

Victor Hugo wrote in *Les Miserables* (Book 5, Chapter 4):

> God is behind everything, but everything hides God.

If God were to reveal Himself to you in all of His universe creating omnipotent glory brighter than a trillion trillion suns, in His terrifying justice, indescribable beauty and irresistible love, your response, if you didn't melt, would be instantaneous and involuntary.

You would collapse like the Apostle John in the Book of Revelation 1:17 "and when I saw him, I fell at his feet as dead"; or I Kings 8:11: "The priests could not stand to minister because of the cloud: for the glory of the LORD had filled the house"; or Ezekiel 3:15 "I sat ... astonished among them seven days."

Every atom of your being would instantly be compelled to fall flat before Him, overriding your free will, and He would know your reaction was an instinctive response to His awesomeness and not a voluntary love response.

> For our God is a consuming fire.
> (Hebrews 12:29; Deuteronomy 4:24)

The angels in the very presence of Almighty God cry out "holy, holy, holy," which in essence is "wow, wow, wow!"

> Holy, holy, holy is the LORD
> Almighty; the whole earth is full of
> his glory. (Isaiah 6:3)

> Holy, holy, holy is the Lord
> God Almighty, who was, and is, and
> is to come. (Revelation 4:8)

Think of it this way, if the Earth were right next to the Sun, you would not be given a choice to see color. You would be blinded by the white-hot bright light. But at a distance of 93 million miles from the Sun, you are allowed to distinguish between all the colors of the rainbow.

Our normal mental state is, in a sense, distant from the awareness of God's presence, thus allowing to us a free will opportunity to choose Him. People say, if God exists, why doesn't He just reveal Himself? Well, if He did, it would not only remove your doubts, it would remove your free will! His omnipotence would overwhelm your senses and you would respond involuntarily!

Another important understanding is this:
— the same condition of God hiding Himself
behind His creation that allows us to have free
will also creates the condition that necessitates
that we have faith:

> For he who comes to God must
> believe that He is, and that He is a
> rewarder of those who diligently
> seek Him. (Hebrews 11:6)

We must daily live in faith that He exists,
though we cannot see Him, trusting in His
promises for what we cannot see:

> Now faith is the substance of things
> hoped for, the evidence of things not seen.
> (Hebrews 11:1)

> While we look not at the things
> which are seen, but at the things which
> are not seen: for the things which are seen
> are temporal; but the things which are not
> seen are eternal. (2 Corinthians 4:18)

> That the trial of your faith, being
> much more precious than of gold that
> perisheth, though it be tried with fire,
> might be found unto praise and honor
> and glory at the appearing of Jesus Christ:
> Whom having not seen, ye love; in whom,
> though now ye see him not, yet believing,
> ye rejoice with joy unspeakable and full
> of glory. (I Peter 1:7-8)

> Without faith it is impossible to please him. (Hebrews 11:6)

> Faith comes by hearing, and hearing by the word of God. (Romans 10:17)

19th century novelist George MacDonald, who inspired C.S. Lewis, J.R.R. Tolkien, and G.K. Chesterton, stated:

> Doubts are the messengers of the Living One to the honest. They are the first knock at our door of things that are not yet, but have to be, understood ...

> Doubts must precede every deeper assurance; for uncertainties are what we first see when we look into a region hitherto unknown, unexplored, unannexed ...

> Any faith in Him, however small, is better than any belief about Him, however great ... A perfect faith would lift us absolutely above fear.

Another aspect of hiding is to prove our love. For example, a recurring theme of love stories is the girl pushing the guy away, but if he refuses to get discouraged and continues to pursue her in hopes of winning her heart, he proves his love. She becomes convinced that his love is genuine. When you run from God and push Him away, He pursues you over and over again, throughout your entire life, wanting a relationship with you. He proves His love for you is genuine.

In a similar way, there are seasons when God hides Himself to see if you will seek after Him. 2 Chronicles 32:31 told of Hezekiah:: "God left him, to try him, that He might know all that was in his heart." Will you prove your love to Him, even when you do not see Him?

> Although the fig tree shall not blossom, neither shall fruit be in the vines ... Yet I will rejoice in the Lord, I will joy in the God of my salvation. (Habakkuk 3:17-18)

♦

A CENTI-BILLIONAIRE'S SON

A handful of individuals on Earth are centi-billionaires – having a net worth of over $100 billion. Imagine if one of their sons went off to college, flying in on his private jet, driving onto campus in a Lamborghini, wearing the finest clothes, gold rings and a Rolex watch, and walking to class followed by an entourage.

He would have every girl fawning over him, wanting to meet him.

But if he hid his immense wealth, laid aside his treasure and position, and drove up to campus in a beat-up old clunker, wearing thread-bare jeans with holes, and sat in the back of class — the uppity girls would ignore him.

But a sweet girl meets him, and they become friends. They like to study together in the library and sit together in the cafeteria.

She is shunned by the in-clique for associating with this nobody guy. They make fun of her and try to embarrass her by saying he would never amount to anything, but she believes in him. He defends her and promises to provide for her.

Despite their mocking, she falls in love with him, and they get engaged. Then one day he says, I want to take you back home to meet my dad. As they drive up to this enormous estate, through the gates up to the entrance of the castle mansion, the girl is blown away and turns to him and says, "Woah!!! You didn't tell me about all of this!" He knows that she loves him for him, not because of all his stuff!

Jesus hid His glory and was born in a lowly stable.

> He grew up before him like a tender shoot, and like a root out of dry ground. He had no beauty or majesty to attract us to him, nothing in his appearance that we should desire him. (Isaiah 53:2 NIV)

He only wants those who choose to love Him for Him.

♦

DEFAULT SETTING OF HUMANITY IS SELFISHNESS

From the moment Adam and Eve sinned, every child born after them was at a distance from God's presence, having, in a sense, a default setting of self-seeking selfishness, a preset magnetic pull towards sin. Why did God allow this? Well, if the normal condition of man is away from God, then it requires an intentional act of one's will to choose God. Otherwise, half the people would be in heaven out of random chance.

As we yield to God's grace, His presence increases, and like an overpowering magnet, breaks us away from the weaker human default attraction towards sin. Thus, the more we seek Him, the more He draws us closer, the more He reveals Himself, pulling us away from temptation.

> Draw nigh to God, and he will draw nigh to you. (James 4:8)

> Turn ye unto me, saith the Lord of hosts, and I will turn unto you. (Zechariah 1:3)

If you seek the Lord with all your heart, He will touch your heart with His love. You will never be the same. The Holy Spirit fills you and you cannot help but think about the love of God. Temptation to sin grows weaker.

Sinning is choosing to love something else more than God. David wrote "Against Thee, Thee only, have I sinned." (Psalm 51:4) Jesus told Peter "Pray, that ye enter not into temptation." When you pray, you are in the presence of the Lord and you will think less about sinning against Him.

♦

GOD CANNOT DENY HIMSELF

What happens if people choose to commit selfish sins? They put God in the position of either having to judge them or deny His just nature by not judging them:

> Now the word of the Lord came to Samuel, saying, "I greatly regret that I have set up Saul as king, for he has turned back from following Me, and has not performed My commandments." (I Samuel 15:10-11)

Let us consider this a little deeper. God loves everything He created. Other than men and angels, creatures are not self-aware and respond in an innocent way. In a sense, they are just acting instinctively in the way God designed them to behave.

Angels are created with free will, but as mentioned earlier, their response to God is never described with the word "love." They are constantly aware that if they willfully sin against God, even one time, He would have to immediately judge them, for if He did not judge them, by default He would be giving consent to their sin, as in law *silence equals consent.* (This is discussed in a later chapter.)

If God gave consent to even one sin one time, He would deny His just nature – He would deny Himself, and "God cannot deny Himself" (2 Timothy 2:13). This means that for all of eternity past, before God created man, He loved everything He created, but His just nature precluded Him from ever being loved back.

But the Father had a plan, before He created anything. In fact, the plan was *the reason* He created everything. "The mystery which was kept secret since the world began" (Romans 16:25). The plan of redemption is His way to love us without having to judge us. He can maintain His unchangeable just nature and love us, and us love Him back, for the rest of eternity, without Him having to judge us, because Jesus took the judgment in our place.

This plan required His only begotten Son to become Emmanuel–God with us, "the Word was made flesh, and dwelt among us" (John 1:14). "Then I said, 'Behold, I have come— In the volume of the book it is written of Me— To do Your will, O God.'" (Hebrews 10:7)

As a man, Jesus would take the judgment we deserved, for only in the flesh could God hang on a tree and die to redeem us.

Charles Wesley wrote the line in his famous hymn, published in 1738:

> Amazing love! How can it be, That
> Thou, my God, shouldst die for me?

On the cross, Jesus was judged as our substitute, "to give his life as a ransom for many." (Mark 10:45) This way, God the Father could maintain His just nature, judging every sin, but He display his loving nature by providing the Lamb to take the judgment for our sins. "For God so loved the world, that he gave his only begotten Son." (John 3:16)

In this was manifested the love of God towards us, because that God sent his only begotten Son into the world, that we might live through him ... He loved us, and sent his Son to be the propitiation for our sins. (I John 4:9-10)

Romans 8:3 states "For what the Law could not do ... God did: sending His own Son in the likeness of sinful flesh and as an offering for sin."

Jesus rose from the dead with a glorified body proving He was who He said He was, and extending the offer to whosoever will believe:

Whosoever believeth in Him shall receive remission of sins. (Acts 10:43)

Whosoever believeth in Him should not perish, but have everlasting life. (John 3:16)

Whosoever shall call upon the name of the Lord shall be saved. (Romans 10:13)

Whosoever liveth and believeth in me shall never die. (John 11:26)

Whosoever will, let him take the water of life freely. (Revelation 22:17)

Whosoever shall confess that Jesus is the Son of God, God dwelleth in him, and he in God. (I John 4:15)

If we slip up and sin, we can trust in the blood of Jesus to cleanse us. I John 1:9 is referred to as a "maintenance verse" as it is to be used often — "If we confess our sins, he is faithful and just to forgive us our sins, and to cleanse us from all unrighteousness."

Confessing is an act of humility. "God resists the proud but gives grace to the humble" (James 4:6); and "His mercies never fail. They are new every morning." (Lamentations 3:23)

To repeat, the Lamb was God's way to love us without having to judge us. The judgment we deserved was placed on Christ. For all eternity we can experience God's perfect love towards us, and we can love Him back without fear of being judged.

I John 4:17-19 states:

> Herein is our love made perfect, that we may have boldness in the day of judgment: because as he is, so are we in this world.
>
> There is no fear in love; but perfect love casteth out fear: because fear hath torment. He that feareth is not made perfect in love. We love him, because he first loved us.

♦

ADAM AND EVE HID

Let us examine further God's plan of redemption. When Adam and Eve sinned against God, they hid. Have you ever sinned against anyone? You really don't want to be around the person you have sinned against. Imagine talking about someone behind their back, laughing about them, joking and making fun of them, and then you look up – and see that very person walking towards you!

Question: Are you drawn to want to go over to that person or do you suddenly feel awkward and embarrassed? You look for an excuse to slip out another way.

It is like two magnets that are stuck together, and one of them turns in the opposite direction. What happens? It repels. The first magnet still wants to connect, but the second one wants to get away.

When Adam and Eve sinned against God, they hid. God still wanted to walk with them in the garden, but they wanted to get away. In other words, it is not so much that God sends sinners to hell, instead, when people sin against God, it is their own consciences make them want to stay away from Him for days, weeks, years, a lifetime! When we sin, our guilty consciences make us want to avoid being alone in God's presence.

As a way of illustration, if you are an honest employee and your boss says, "I want to see you in my office." No problem, you go in. But if you have been coming in late, taking extended lunches, not doing your job, cheating, or stealing from the company ... do you want to go into your boss's office? No! You dread it. You are fearful, nervous, and apprehensive.

Or if you are driving the speed limit and

see a police car, it is no big deal. But if you have been speeding and see the police, your heart beats faster, you sweat, you cannot wait to get far enough away so that you no longer see him in the rear-view mirror. Even children avoid looking into the eyes of their parents when they are lying. This reaction was seen in the Gospel of John, chapter 8:

> Pharisees brought unto Jesus a woman taken in adultery … "Moses in the law commanded us, that such should be stoned: but what sayest thou?" … He lifted up himself, and said unto them, "He that is without sin among you, let him first cast a stone at her."

> And again he stooped down, and wrote·on the ground. And they which heard it, being convicted by their own conscience, went out one by one, beginning at the eldest, even unto the last.

In the presence of Jesus, they became aware of their sins and wanted to get away. When Jesus cast demons out of a man of the Gadarenes, the locals, knowing they were sinners, responded:

> Then the whole multitude of the surrounding region of the Gadarenes asked Him to depart from them, for they were seized with great fear. (Luke 8:36-37)

Even Peter, when Jesus caused a miraculous catch of fish, felt this impulse:

> And they came and filled both
> the boats, so that they began to
> sink. When Simon Peter saw it, he
> fell down at Jesus' knees, saying,
> "Depart from me, for I am a sinful
> man, O Lord!" (Luke 5:7-8)

When Adam and Eve sinned against God, they hid from Him.

◆

ADAM & EVE'S RELIGION OF FIG LEAVES

Realizing they blew it, Adam and Eve came up with the idea of doing something to make themselves acceptable to God again. They put on fig leaves.

This was the beginning of false religions: men and women coming up with their own ideas of how to make themselves acceptable to God. It was a religion of doing things – a religion of works.

Did Adam and Eve's fig leaves make them acceptable to God? No. Then we read this line:

> Unto Adam also and to his wife
> did the LORD God make coats of skins
> and clothed them. (Genesis 3:21)

We read it quickly, but if you think of it, how does one make a coat of skin? Something has to die! Do you think God went to the other side of the Garden, killed an animal, and brought Adam and Eve some nice, tailored outfits? Or do you think maybe He killed the animal right in front of them, and Adam and Eve witnessed the first death ever, since this would have been the first thing to die after the Biblical creation account?

Imagine Adam and Eve watching in dismay as this innocent animal went through the pangs of dying, thinking to themselves, we are the ones who sinned, but this innocent animal is the one who is dying.

Then God wanted to make it so clear the animal died in their place, that right in front of them, He stripped the skin off the animal and put it on their naked bodies. Maybe it still had some blood on it. They were "covered in the blood of the Lamb."

For the rest of their lives, Adam and Eve wore the skin of the animal that they watched die in their place. And whenever God looked upon Adam and Eve, He saw them clothed with the skin of this animal – "the Lamb slain from the foundations of the world." (Revelation 13:8)

This was the original foreshadowing of Jesus' atonement on the cross. "Unto him that loved us and washed us from our sins in his own blood." (Revelation 1:5)

♦

CAIN'S RELIGION OF WORKS

Adam and Eve certainly told their experience to their sons, Cain and Abel, who, when they became adults, decided to worship God.

Now Abel was a keeper of

sheep, while Cain was a tiller of the soil. So in the course of time, Cain brought some of the fruit of the soil as an offering to the LORD, while Abel brought the best portions of the firstborn of his flock. (Genesis 4)

What Cain did was similar to the fig leaf religion, the idea of doing things to make one acceptable to God. It is clear that Cain's was a "religion of works," because God had told Adam:

Cursed is the ground because of you; through toil you will eat of it all the days of your life. Both thorns and thistles it will yield for you, and you will eat the plants of the field. By the sweat of your brow you will eat your bread. (Genesis 3:19)

Sweat is work. It can be imagined that Cain sweat as he weeded out "thorns and thistles" to bring forth "plants of the field." In other words, Cain was attempting to earn his way to heaven. He was trusting in his own efforts.

Did Cain's works make him acceptable to God? No. Abel, on the other hand, offered the sacrifice of "the firstborn of his flock."

And the LORD looked with favor on Abel and his offering, but He had no regard for Cain and his offering. So Cain became very angry, and his countenance fell. (Genesis 4:4-5)

Cain's offering was one of works. When

someone does works, they can be proud of their works. When Cain's works were rejected, "his countenance fell," his pride was hurt, he was embarrassed in front of his family. Some people will not come to the Lord because they care too much about what their family and friends will think about them. This is pride, the sin of Satan. Cain took offense, became angry, hateful, and finally murdered his brother.

Abel's trusting in the Lamb was an implicit acknowledgment that he was insufficient in himself, that he needed help—he was humble.

In Luke 18: 9-14, Jesus described two men who prayed: a pharisee and a publican. The pharisee was proud while the publican was humble. The publican "went to his house justified" while the pharisee did not. Jesus concluded "For everyone that exalteth himself shall be abased; and he that humbleth himself shall be exalted."

> God opposes the proud, but gives grace to the humble. Humble yourselves, therefore, under God's mighty hand, so that in due time He may exalt you. (I Peter 5:5-6)

The situation is this: God is on one side; we are on the other side; our sins have separated us from God (Isaiah 59:2); and the Lamb paid for our sins. (John 1:29)

The Lamb took the judgment for our unjust sins so we could be accepted by a just God. Jesus did not get rid of the Law, He simply paid the penalty for us breaking it. Abel's sacrifice foreshadowed the atonement – at one moment God and man are reconciled.

◆

MIRROR, SOAP AND WATER

Two important themes stand out when reading through the Pentateuch–the first five books of the Bible, namely: the Law, and the sacrifices to be offered when one breaks the Law. James described the Law as a mirror:

> For if anyone is a hearer of the word and not a doer, he is like a man who looks intently at his natural face in a mirror … and goes away and at once forgets what he was like. (James 1:23-25 ESV)

A bathroom has a mirror, and soap and water. The mirror shows you how dirty your face is, but it has no power to cleanse your face. It does, though, create the desire within you to wash with the soap and the water.

You think you are a pretty good person? Look into the mirror and try to keep the Law for a while. Oh, yes, and it is one strike and you're out! All you have to do is sin one time in your entire life and you can never go to heaven by being good enough.

> For whoever shall keep the whole law, and yet stumble in one point, he is guilty of all. (James 2:10)

> By the works of the Law no flesh will be justified in His sight;

for through the Law comes the knowledge of sin. (Romans 3:20)

Woah! If that is the case, I need help!

Fine. Now that I have your attention, here is help. 1 John 1:7 states: "The blood of Jesus his Son cleanses us from all sin."

These are the ones coming out of the great tribulation. They have washed their robes and made them white in the blood of the Lamb. (Revelation 7:13-14)

The mirror shows us we are sinners but it has no power to cleanse us of our sin. It does, though, serve a purpose. It creates the desire in us to use the soap and water. The Law show us our need for the Lamb.

And almost all things are by the law purged with blood; and without shedding of blood is no remission. (Hebrew 9:22)

Rev. Billy Graham wrote:

The Bible teaches that the law was given as a mirror. When we look into God's Word, we see what true righteousness is ... The law exposes our sin and shows us our true spiritual condition. Such a mirror does not reveal a very attractive image!

Sin had to be paid for, so in the beginning God instituted the sacrificial system ... In Old Testament times, those who had sinned brought sacrifices of animals and offered them to God. This foreshadowed the Great Sacrifice yet to come.

St. Augustine wrote:

> The law orders that we, after attempting to do what is ordered, and so feeling our weakness under the law, may learn to implore the help of grace.

♦

OLD TESTAMENT SACRIFICES POINT TO JESUS

Old Testament believers had faith in the Lamb to come, just as New Testament believers have faith in the Lamb that came, but salvation is only through the Lamb.

Believers understand that the sacrifice is their substitute, that it died in their place, that its shed blood would somehow make them acceptable to God. (Leviticus 17:11)

In the Old Testament, whatever the animal was, be it a lamb, goat, ox, or dove, its shed blood was a foreshadowing of Jesus' sacrifice on the cross.

NOAH offered "clean animals" when he got off the ark. (Genesis 8:20)

ABRAHAM cut animals in half for the Lord to walk between when He entered into covenant. (Genesis 15:6-10) After years of trusting God's promise that he would have a son, the Lord visited Abraham, who killed a

lamb for a meal. Afterwards, the Lord told him
Sarah would conceive Isaac. (Genesis 18:7-8)
Then, when Isaac was a young man:

> It came to pass after these
> things that God tested Abraham ...
> and said ... "Take now your son, your
> only son Isaac, whom you love, and
> go to the land of Moriah, and offer
> him there as a burnt offering on one
> of the mountains of which I shall tell
> you." (Genesis 22:1-2)

Abraham obeyed. He trusted in God's
promise that through Isaac his descendants
would be as the stars of the heavens. Abraham
believed God would keep His promise, even
if that meant resurrecting Isaac after he was
sacrificed. Hebrews 11:17-19 states:

> By faith Abraham, when he was
> tested, offered up Isaac, and he who
> had received the promises offered up
> his only begotten son, of whom it was
> said, "In Isaac your seed shall be called,"
> concluding that God was able to raise him
> up, even from the dead, from which he
> also received him in a figurative sense.

ISAAC was willing to be sacrificed. God
stopped Abraham and showed him that he
should instead sacrifice a substitute – a ram
caught by his head in a thorn bush, a symbolic
foreshadowing of Christ, whose head was
crowned with thorns. (Genesis 22:6-14)

JACOB, following the instruction of his mother Rebekah, sought to deceive his father Isaac in order to get his older brother's blessing. He killed a lamb for stew, then wearing his brother's clothes, and the wool of the lamb over the back of his neck and back of his hands, carried the lamb stew to his father, whose eyesight was failing. Isaac, thinking Jacob was his brother, gave him the blessing of the firstborn. (Genesis 27:6-29)

The symbolism is that God blesses us not because of us, for we are deceitful sinners. We approach God wearing the righteousness of our older brother, Jesus, trusting in Him as the Lamb of God, and our heavenly Father blesses us for Jesus' sake.

MOSES had every family in Israel kill a lamb and put the blood over the door posts of their house so that the Angel of Death, executing the judgment of God, would "pass over." The blood displayed that those inside were trusting that the lamb was slain in their place. (Exodus 12:3-11)

SAMSON'S parents offered a sacrifice. (Judges 13:15-23)

SAMUEL the Prophet offered sacrifices, after which the Lord thundered, and the Philistines were defeated. (I Samuel 7:9-12) Samuel also offered sacrifices at Gilgal. (I Samuel 11:15)

ELIJAH confronted the prophets of Baal at Mount Carmel by putting a sacrifice on the altar, drenching it with water, then calling upon the Lord, who showed He accepted it by sending fire from heaven to consume it. (I Kings 18:30-39)

DAVID offered sacrifices when he brought the Ark into Jerusalem. (2 Samuel 6:12-13) He offered sacrifices at Araunah's threshing floor on the top of Mount Moriah to stop a plague. (1 Chronicles 21:24-26) That spot became the Temple Mount.

SOLOMON offered thousands of sacrifices when he dedicated the Temple. When one approached the Temple, the first thing seen was the altar.

JOHN THE BAPTIST pointed at Jesus and said, "Behold the LAMB OF GOD who taketh away the sins of the world." (John 1:29)

This was a reference to the Day of Atonement described in Leviticus 16. The HIGH PRIEST took two young goats (the Hebrew word *seh* means lamb or goat) and placed them before the congregation of the people. The one on which the Lord's lot fell was the spotless sacrifice. The High Priest offered it on behalf of the sinful nation, then carried its blood through the Holy Place into the Holy of Holies. Leviticus 16:15-16:

> Then shall Aaron (the High Priest) kill the goat of the sin offering, that is for the people, and bring his blood within the veil ... and sprinkle it upon the mercy seat ... And he

shall make an atonement for ... the
children of Israel ... because of their
transgressions in all their sins.

The mercy seat was the golden lid of the
Ark of the Covenant, where two golden angels
had their wings stretched towards each other
with the presence of the Lord between them.

Inside the Ark were the two stone tablets
engraved with the Ten Commandments.
The blood sprinkled on the mercy seat was
between the presence of the Lord above and
presence of the Law below. This represented
the blood covering the sins of the people.

Booker T. Washington wrote in *Putting the
Most into Life* (NY: Thomas Crowell & Co.,
1906, "Making Religion a Vital Part of Living"):

The word "atonement," which occurs
in the Bible again and again, means literally
at-one-ment. To be at one with God.

Had the High Priest approached the
presence of the Lord without the blood, he
would have been approaching the "judgment
seat" of God, as the people deserved judgment.
The sprinkled blood actually changed it from
a "judgment seat" into a "mercy seat."

Since there was no lamp in the Holy of
Holies, the presence of the Lord between the
two golden angels was the only light, and it
would have shown continually like a spotlight
on the blood sprinkled on the mercy seat.

Isaiah, chapter 53, described the Messiah
as the sacrificed Lamb:

Surely he took up our pain and bore our suffering, yet we considered him punished by God, stricken by him, and afflicted. But he was pierced for our transgressions, he was crushed for our iniquities; the punishment that brought us peace was on him, and by his wounds we are healed ...

The Lord has laid on him the iniquity of us all. He was oppressed and afflicted, yet he did not open his mouth; he was led like a lamb to the slaughter, and as a sheep before its shearers is silent ...

He was cut off from the land of the living; for the transgression of my people he was punished ... Yet it was the Lord's will to crush him and cause him to suffer ... The Lord makes his life an offering for sin ...

My righteous servant will justify many, and he will bear their iniquities ... For he bore the sin of many and made intercession for the transgressors.

To make it unmistakably clear what just happened with the atonement, the High Priest laid his hands on the head of the second goat which escaped being killed—the "escapegoat," and confessed the sins of the nation over it so as to identify it with the sinful people which just escaped judgment. It was taken by the hand of a young man far away and let go free.

It was let go in the wilderness where it could never find its way back, symbolizing the guilt of those sins would never return.

> As far as the east is from the west, so far has he removed our transgressions from us. (Psalm 103:13)

All four Gospels tell how both Jesus and Barabbas stood before the congregation of the people. Pilate declared Jesus innocent. He was the spotless Lamb. The priests chose Him to be sacrificed. John 11 recorded:

> Caiaphas ... the High Priest ... said ... it is expedient for us, that one man should die for the people, and that the whole nation perish not. And this spake he not of himself: but being High Priest that year, he prophesied that Jesus should die for that nation; And not for that nation only ...

Jesus' blood was shed to make atonement for the sins of the world. Barabbas, the guilty criminal, escaped judgment and was let go free. Barabbas represents all of us sinners who escaped judgment and are set free because Jesus was our substitute.

> Having erased the charges that were brought against us ... when he nailed them to the cross. (Colossians 2:14)

> The Lord sets the prisoners free. (Psalm 146:7)

To reiterate, Old Testament believers had faith in the Lamb *to come*; New Testament believers have faith in the Lamb *that came*; but for both, salvation is through the Lamb.

> Jesus saith unto him, I am the way,
> the truth, and the life: no man cometh
> unto the Father, but by me. (John 14:6)

All prophecies require an element of faith, as "without faith it is impossible to please God." (Hebrews 11:6)

Early believers were Jews. Jews do not "convert" in the sense that they do not leave their Jewishness to become believers. Gentiles are the ones who convert to believing in Jewish scriptures. Jews simply come to believe in their own scriptures – that the prophecies regarding the Messiah were fulfilled in Jesus.

◆

GOD IS JUST AND HE CANNOT CHANGE HIS NATURE

In a mathematical equation, there are variables and constants. Variables can change, but a constant is a value that never changes. God's just nature is a constant. It never changes. And for Him to be just He must judge every sin.

In the equation of redemption, the variable is who gets judged, you or a substitute. Another variable is when. Is the judgment now, which many wish for their enemies but not for themselves; in the future; or in the past, trusting in the judgment Jesus took upon

Himself on the cross in our place.

God was, is, and forever will be just. "For I am the LORD, I change not" (Malachi 3:6); "All His ways are justice" (Deuteronomy 32:4); "For I the LORD love justice" (Isaiah 61:8); Abraham proclaimed, "Shall not the Judge of all the earth deal justly?" (Genesis 18:25) God is just and He cannot help it. "He cannot deny Himself." (2 Timothy 2:13)

Sir William Blackstone wrote in *Commentaries on the Laws of England,* (1765-69):

> The Creator ... has laid down only such laws as were founded in those relations of justice ... These are the eternal, immutable laws of good and evil, to which the Creator Himself in all his dispensations conforms; and which He has enabled human reason to discover ...

> The Creator is a Being, not only of infinite power, and wisdom, but also of infinite goodness, He has so intimately connected ... the laws of eternal justice with the happiness of each individual, that the latter cannot be attained but by observing the former.

As mentioned earlier, a maxim in common law is that "silence gives consent." It is called the *rule of tacit admission.* Remember in wedding ceremonies how the minister would ask if anyone was present who objected, that they should "speak now or forever hold their peace." If you are there, silent, holding your peace, you are giving consent.

Silence equals consent is in Numbers 30:

> If a daughter makes a vow to the Lord, and binds herself by some agreement while in her father's house in her youth, and her father hears her vow and ... holds his peace, then all her vows shall stand ... But if her father overrules her on the day that he hears, then none of her vows ... shall stand.

If there are sins, and God is silent and does not judge them, by default, He would effectively be giving consent to the sin, and if He gives consent to sin, He is no longer a just God. To ask God to simply overlook a sin without judging it is to ask Him to deny His just nature – to deny Himself, which He cannot do, as "God cannot deny Himself." (2 Timothy 2:13) He has to keep His Word. Hebrews 6:18 "It is impossible for God to lie"; Titus 1:2 "God, who cannot lie."

If God lied, He would be submitting Himself to the devil, who is the father of liars, as Jesus rebuked the Pharisees in John 8:44:

> Ye are of your father the devil ... there is no truth in him. When he speaketh a lie, he speaketh of his own: for he is a liar, and the father of it.

Therefore, for God to be true to His nature,

He cannot lie, He must be truthful, He must keep His Word, He must be just and judge every sin, even the tiniest, for it is not the quantity but the quality. It is not the size of a sin that matters but the nature of it. Its essence is evil.

Whether a lot or a little, you won't eat garbage because the nature of is garbage. You judge it unworthy to be accepted not because of the amount of it but because its essence is rotten.

♦

HE IS A GOD OF JUSTICE—YET HE WANTS YOUR LOVE

God created everything with rules. He is an eternal, perfect, all powerful, all-knowing Being, who is completely just, with order, laws, and rules.

Richard Feynman, a Nobel Prize winner in quantum electrodynamics, wrote in *The Meaning of It All: Thoughts of a Citizen–Scientist* (NY: BasicBooks, 1998):

> Why nature is mathematical is
> a mystery ... The fact that there are
> rules at all is a kind of miracle.

In 1960, Princeton physicist Eugene Wigner asked why the natural world always obeys the laws of mathematics?:

> The enormous usefulness
> of mathematics in the natural
> sciences is something bordering
> on the mysterious and there is

no rational explanation for it. ("The Unreasonable Effectiveness of Mathematics in the Natural Sciences," *Mathematics,* 1984)

A picture of how God created everything with rules is seen in how man created computers. At their most basic level, they operate with exact rules. There are two magnetic charges, on and off, written in binary computer language as 0 and 1.

Upon the strict arrangements of 0 and 1 are built machine codes, then software, then all of the amazing programs and apps which we use every day.

So it is with creation. God made the smallest subatomic particles, then assembled them in a precise order, following rules and laws, such as: Law of Quantum Physics, Mathematics, Energy Conservation, Gravity, Thermodynamics, Entropy, Chemistry, Biology, Planetary Motion, Nature, etc.

Everything He created follows laws. Animals are programmed to follow rules, called instinct. These instincts determine how they interact with each other.

God also has completely fair and just rules for human interaction. We just have the choice whether or not to follow them. If we break His rules it is called "sin."

To summarize, God loves you and wants you to love Him back. He does not need your love, but He wants it. Love must be voluntary.

If it is forced, it evaporates. God gives us free will, but if we sin against Him, He must judge us or else He would be giving consent to our sin and denying His just nature, denying Himself.

So He had a plan – He would provide the sacrifice to take the judgment for our sins so we could approach Him without fear of judgment. We just have to have faith in the sacrifice He provided.

◆

FOR GOD TO BE JUST HE HAS TO JUDGE EVERY SIN

Since we are made in God's image, the desire for justice has been implanted in every one of us. Every child knows it is unfair for one child to get more toys and candy than another.

Nearly every police drama on television, like NCIS, starts off with an injustice done in the first two minutes – some innocent person is killed. And you are held captive the rest of the hour wanting the person who did it to be caught and brought to justice. Something inside of you knows that the criminal needs to pay, that the sin must be judged.

In the first two minutes of the Book of Genesis, an injustice is done. Cain killed Abel. The Lord said to Cain (Genesis 4:8-10): "What have you done? The voice of your brother's blood cries out to Me from the ground."

What was it crying? An injustice was done – an innocent person was killed – You are a just God, You have to judge the one who did it. The Contemporary English Version words it: "his blood is calling out for me to punish you."

This is the only side of God that the devil knew. Originally, Satan was Lucifer, the most beautiful angel, but he became puffed up with pride and wanted to put himself higher than the throne of God. Jesus said in John 8:44:

Ye are of your father the devil ...

He was a murderer from the beginning.

Satan convinced a third of the angels to rebel with him. (Revelations 12:3-9) God's response was, you have sinned against me, you are judged and cast out of my presence! (Isaiah 14:12-19; Ezekiel 28:12-19; Revelation 12:7-9)

It was like a massive electric circuit-breaker of universal scale suddenly flipped. Satan's polarity changed, and in an instant, he was shot out of heaven like an electrical short, a blown fuse. Jesus said, "I saw Satan fall from Heaven like lightning." (Luke 10:18)

♦

WHY DID THE LAMB HAVE TO DIE?

Satan was cast down to Earth and came into the Garden of Eden. There he saw Adam and Eve, and thought to himself, if I can tempt Adam and Eve to sin against God, even just one time, then God will have to judge them.

Satan got them to sin, that was easy, then he stood back and accused God by saying in essence — they sinned against you, you have to judge them, for if you do not, your silence is giving consent to their sin, and if you give consent to sin, you are no longer a just God, you deny your just nature, you deny yourself, you forgo your right to rule, you effectively ungod yourself, you are kicked out of heaven!

Satan made a similar accusation in Job 1:6-12, accusing God of being an unjust "respecter of persons" who blessed and protected Job more than others. If God were to show partiality, He would be breaking His own Law, as Leviticus 19:15 states "You shall do no injustice in judgment. You shall not be partial to the poor, nor honor the person of the mighty." God spent the next forty-two chapters of the Book of Job showing He is not a respecter of persons.

But God did judge Adam and Eve's sin. He sent, in a sense, a fireball of judgment down, but to the dismay of Satan, in stepped the Lamb to take the hit. This way, God could remain just, in that He judges every sin, but God is love, in that He provided the Lamb to take the judgment for the sin.

♦

GOD WILL PROVIDE HIMSELF A LAMB

When Abraham was taking his son, Isaac, to the top of Mount Moriah:

> Isaac spake unto Abraham his father, and said, My father: and he said, Here am I, my son. And he said, Behold the fire and the wood:

> but where is the lamb for a burnt
> offering? And Abraham said, My
> son, God will provide himself a lamb
> for a burnt offering. (Genesis 22:7-8)

This passage has a double meaning: first —that God will provide a sacrifice, —a ram caught by its head in a thorn bush on top of Mount Moriah; and second —that God will provide Himself as the sacrifice.

And that is what happened. Jesus, the second person of the Trinity, the only begotten Son of God, became the sacrifice. It was a covenant—Abraham did not withhold his only promised son, but was willing to sacrifice him, and God the Father did not withhold His only Son and did sacrifice Him.

♦

JESUS ALWAYS KNEW THE PLAN

Jesus knew that it was His Father's plan for Him to be the sacrificed Lamb.

> And he took again the twelve, and
> began to tell them what things should
> happen unto him, Saying, Behold, we
> go up to Jerusalem; and the Son of man
> shall be delivered unto the chief priests,
> and unto the scribes; and they shall
> condemn him to death, and shall deliver
> him to the Gentiles: And they shall mock
> him, and shall scourge him, and shall
> spit upon him, and shall kill him: and
> the third day he shall rise again. (Mark
> 10:32-34; Luke 18:31-33)

He then began to teach them that the Son of Man must suffer many things and be rejected by the elders, the chief priests and the teachers of the law, and that he must be killed and after three days rise again. (Mark 8:31)

For he taught his disciples ... "The Son of man is delivered into the hands of men, and they shall kill him; and after that he is killed, he shall rise the third day." Mark 9:31

Jesus called them together and said ... The Son of Man did not come to be served, but to serve, and to give his life as a ransom for many. (Mark 10:42-45)

Now is my soul troubled; and what shall I say? Father, save me from this hour: but for this cause came I unto this hour. (John 12:27)

Then said Jesus unto Peter, "Put up thy sword into the sheath: the cup which my Father hath given me, shall I not drink it?" (John 18:11)

♦

BOOK OF REVELATION JUDGMENT

How was Jesus' sacrifice sufficient to pay for all of our sins? To understand this, we need to consider the Book of Revelation. It is difficult to understand, but one thing seems clear, it is God who is pouring out the vials of judgment. Why is that?

Since God is just, He has to judge every sin He had not judged since the beginning of time. So you can't get ten thousand years into eternity and someone say, God, there was this sin way back when and you did not judge it. Were you silent? Were you giving consent to the sin? Is there a part of you that is unjust that we didn't know about?

NO. Absolutely not. The Book of Revelation 14:11 states:

> The smoke of their torment rises forever and forever.

And Revelation 16:7 states:

> And I heard another voice from the altar saying, "Even so, Lord God Almighty, true and righteous are Your judgments."

Nobody will question for the rest of eternity that God judged sin. But since this is the Final Judgment, He will not have to do any more judging for the rest of eternity!

Skeptics say, how could there be a God if there are injustices in the world. One should not confuse God's patience with injustice. Just because He is long-suffering, offering every possible opportunity for sinners to repent, does not mean He won't eventually judge the wicked deeds done by sinners who choose not to repent. Romans 9:22 stated:

What if God, although fully intending to show [the awfulness of] His wrath and to make known His power and authority, has tolerated with much patience the vessels (objects) of [His] anger which are ripe for destruction?

God's patience and long-suffering does not mean eternal tolerance. 2 Peter 3:9 states:

The Lord is not slack concerning his promise, as some men count slackness; but is long-suffering to us-ward, not willing that any should perish, but that all should come to repentance.

At the Final Judgment He will finally judge every evil atrocity, horrendous genocide, rape, murder, kidnapping, sex-trafficking, molestation, murder, and ungodly act that has not been judged since the beginning of time.

But in this sense, the equivalent of the Book of Revelation judgment was poured out on Jesus. He took the judgment for every sin that everybody would ever commit upon Himself on the cross. I John 2:1-2 states:

Jesus Christ ... is the propitiation for our sins: and not for ours only, but also the sins of the whole world.

I Peter 2:24 states:

Who Himself bore our sins in His own body on the tree, that we, having died to sins, might live for righteousness—by whose stripes you were healed.

♦

JESUS WAS JUDGED IN OUR PLACE

1) God has to judge every sin. If He does not judge, His silence is giving consent to the sin, rendering Him unjust; (Hebrews 2:2)

2) For God to be just, He cannot judge one person who sinned more or less than another. He cannot be a respecter of persons (Acts 10:34-35);

3) For a judge to be just, he must require that a thief repay with something of equal or greater value to what was stolen. (Exodus 22:4,7; Proverbs 6:31)

We are like the thief. There are billions of us humans, past and present, and we have all sinned and deserve judgment. Our judgment would be eternal separation from a just God. For Jesus to be our substitute, His suffering needed to be equal to or greater than what all of us combined would have suffered!

Being the eternal Son of God, He experienced the day on the cross in a way we could never imagine: "One day is with the Lord as a thousand years." (II Peter 3:8)

Jesus prayed near the Mount of Olives in the Garden of Gethsemane, which means olive press—where olives were crushed into oil:

> He knelt down and prayed, saying, "Father, if it is Your will, take this cup away from Me; nevertheless not My will, but Yours, be done."

Then an angel appeared to Him from heaven, strengthening Him.

And being in agony, He prayed more earnestly. Then His sweat became like great drops of blood falling down to the ground. (Luke 22:42-44)

He was about to experience the totality of all the judgment deserved by all of humanity.

John Piper of Bethlehem College & Seminary explained (June 12, 2009):

If our sins are punished by eternal separation from God, why did Jesus only have to suffer momentary separation? ...

The answer is that ... our sins are infinitely great because they are against an infinite person and deserve an infinite punishment ...

Christ, being an infinite person, became so low that that drop in suffering, that drop in indignity was such a huge drop—it was an infinite drop—that it suffices to cover the sins of millions and to cover the entire length of eternity that we deserve to be in hell.

♦

JESUS PAID IT ALL

A just scale has to balance. (Proverbs 20:10) God's plan of redemption had to be just — it had to balance.

An ETERNAL BEING who is INNOCENT

suffering for a FINITE period of time is equal to all FINITE beings who are GUILTY suffering for an ETERNAL period of time.

Let us read that again:

An ETERNAL BEING –Jesus, the only-begotten Son of God, – who is INNOCENT, suffering for a FINITE – limited period of time – the day on the cross, is equal to all of us FINITE beings – who are GUILTY sinners, suffering for an ETERNAL period of time.

Another way of putting it is:

An UNLIMITED BEING suffering for a LIMITED period of time is equal to all of us LIMITED BEINGS suffering for an UNLIMITED period of time.

INFINITY times FINITE equals FINITE times INFINITY. His infinitely positive sacrifice canceled out our infinitely negative sins. Isaiah 53:10 "It pleased the Lord to crush him." Jesus single-handedly experienced suffering equivalent to the combined eternal damnation that all of us together deserved. And HE IS THE ONLY ONE WHO COULD HAVE DONE IT!

And for eternity, God the Father will continually see Jesus' sacrifice as if it just happened: "For a thousand years in thy sight are but as yesterday when it is past" (Psalm 90:4); and He will forever remember His Son's dying request "Father, forgive them, for they know not what they do." (Luke 23:34)

What did Jesus experience when He took the judgment for our sins upon Himself on the cross? Matthew 27:46 recorded: "And about the ninth hour Jesus cried with a loud voice, saying, Eli, Eli, lama sabachthani? that is to say, My God, my God, why hast thou forsaken me?"

A prophetic insight is given in Matthew 12, when Jesus replied to those demanding a sign:

> None will be given it except the sign of the prophet Jonah. For as Jonah was three days and three nights in the belly of the great fish, so the Son of Man will be three days and three nights in the heart of the earth.

The Book of Jonah, chapter 2, described:

> Then Jonah prayed unto the Lord his God out of the fish's belly, And said, "I cried by reason of mine affliction unto the Lord, and he heard me; out of the belly of hell cried I, and thou heardest my voice.

> For thou hadst cast me into the deep, in the midst of the seas; and the floods compassed me about: all thy billows and thy waves passed over me.

> Then I said, I am cast out of thy sight; yet I will look again toward thy holy temple. The waters compassed me about, even to the soul: the depth closed me round about, the weeds were wrapped about my head. I went down to the bottoms of the mountains; the earth

with her bars was about me FOREVER: yet hast thou brought up my life from corruption, O Lord my God.

When my soul fainted within me, I remembered the Lord; and my prayer went up to You, into Your holy temple. They that observe lying vanities forsake their own mercy. But I will sacrifice unto thee with the voice of thanksgiving; I will pay that which I have vowed. Salvation is of the Lord." So the Lord spoke to the fish, and it vomited Jonah onto dry land.

In Acts, chapter 2:21-27, Peter proclaimed after the Resurrection:

Ye men of Israel, hear these words; Jesus of Nazareth, a man approved of God among you by miracles and wonders and signs, which God did by him in the midst of you ... being delivered by the determinate counsel and foreknowledge of God, ye have taken, and by wicked hands have crucified and slain:

Whom God hath raised up, having loosed the pains of death: because it was not possible that he should be holden of it. For David speaketh concerning him, "... Thou wilt not leave my soul in hell, neither wilt thou suffer thine Holy One to see corruption."

> Men and brethren, let me freely ... The patriarch David ... being a prophet ... spake of the resurrection of Christ, that his soul was not left in hell, neither his flesh did see corruption. This Jesus hath God raised up, whereof we all are witnesses.

Out of love for the Father, and out of love for you and me, Jesus became the sacrificial Lamb, and then rose from the dead to prove He was who He said He was, so now you and I can enjoy fellowship with God in Heaven for eternity. "For the joy that was set before him endured the cross, despising the shame." (Hebrews 12:2) In His plan, GOD is JUST, in that He judged every sin, but HE is LOVE, in that He provided the Lamb to take the judgment for our sins.

> God for Christ's sake hath forgiven you. (Ephesians 4:32)

Now, Satan lost his job. Satan, which means "accuser," points out your sins to God in an effort to get God to judge you, but God already judged you—in Christ!

> Now is come salvation ... for the accuser of our brethren is cast down, which accused them before our God day and night. And they overcame him by the blood of the

Lamb, and by the word of their testimony. (Revelation 12:10-11)

... and shall not come into judgment, but has passed from death into life. (John 5:24)

... Who hath delivered us from the power of darkness, and hath translated us into the kingdom of his dear Son. (Colossians 1:13)

George Washington Carver wrote to Jack Boyd of the Denver YMCA, March 1, 1927:

Lead others into the realms of true happiness, where a religion of hate, (which poisons both body and soul) will be unknown, having in its place the 'Golden Rule' way, which is the 'Jesus Way' of life,

God, my beloved friend, is infinite, the highest embodiment of love. We are finite, surrounded and often filled with hate. We can only understand the infinite as we loose the finite and take on the infinite.

♦

WE ARE IN CHRIST

In the flat wheat fields of western Kansas, the worst thing that can happen is a hailstorm. You can stand in the field and be hailed upon, or you can run into the barn. You hear the hail hitting the tin roof, but you are safe inside.

Jesus is our barn, the judgment of hail comes, but we are safe in Him.

> He shall cover thee with his
> feathers, and under His wings shalt
> thou trust. (Psalm 91:4)

An insight into what it means to be "in Christ" comes from what Jesus said on the cross: "Father, forgive them, for they know not what they do." (Luke 23:34)

Jesus was completely innocent, yet He was unjustly being crucified by both the Jews and the Gentile Romans. At that instant, God could have justly judged all humanity for killing His innocent Son, and the Book of Revelation judgment would have begun immediately right then. But instead, Jesus called out for God to forgive us. It was like Jesus pressed the pause button on God's judgment.

Jesus is like an umbrella. We are under His covering. He was rained upon to keep us dry. He took the judgment so we would not. He was like Noah's Ark, which endured the torrential flood while we are safe and secure inside. We are "in Christ."

> Romans 8:1 declares: "There
> is therefore now no condemnation
> to them which are in Christ Jesus."

For the next 2,000 years, the Holy Spirit has gathered all who would, to come under the umbrella, to come, as it were, into the Ark of Christ. Finally, when all are in that are going to come in, Jesus releases the pause button, breaks the seal, and God resumes with the final judgment.

Jesus, being completely innocent, is the only one who could break the seal to release the judgment because everyone else has sinned and for them to break the seal would be releasing judgment on their own heads. Revelation, chapter 5 states:

> I saw in the right hand of him who sat on the throne a scroll ... sealed with seven seals. And I saw a mighty angel proclaiming in a loud voice, "Who is worthy to break the seals and open the scroll?" But no one in heaven or on earth or under the earth could open the scroll or even look inside it. I wept ...

> Then one of the elders said to me, "Do not weep! See, the Lion of the tribe of Judah, the Root of David, has triumphed. He is able to open the scroll and its seven seals." Then I saw a Lamb, looking as if it had been slain, standing at the center of the throne, encircled by the four living creatures and the elders ...

> He went and took the scroll from the right hand of him who sat on the throne ... And when he had taken it, the four living creatures and the twenty-four elders fell down before the Lamb ... And they sang a new song, saying: "You are worthy to take the scroll and to

open its seals, because you were slain,
and with your blood you purchased
for God persons from every tribe and
language and people and nation."

God forever sees us through the sacrifice
of Christ. Just as the Temple had daily
sacrifices which were symbolic of Jesus, the
Father for all time, sees Jesus' sacrifice in
His relationship with us, and as a result, He is
ever patient, forgiving and gracious towards us!
Christ Jesus is ever at the right hand of the
Father making intercession for us:

Who is he that condemneth? It
is Christ that died, yea rather, that
is risen again, who is even at the
right hand of God, who also maketh
intercession for us. (Romans 8:34)

♦

ARE YOU LIKE CAIN OR ABEL?

A question can be asked, are you
approaching God as Cain or as Abel?

If you are still trying to be good enough
to go to heaven, you are approaching God as
Cain did, – thinking, I hope I put enough of
my good works on the altar. Maybe a couple
more handfuls of barley will do it.

Or are you approaching God as Abel, –
thinking, It is not me being good enough – it
is the Lamb that was good enough to take the
judgment for all of my sins.

As long as you think your acceptance by

God is based on you being good enough, you will always have this nagging thought in the back of your head – "did I do enough?" And your own conscience will tell you – No, you did not do enough, and you never can, you will always fall short.

That very thought will cause you to hesitate coming into the Lord's presence, questioning yourself, did I do enough, I am not sure, I am uncertain, apprehensive.

> There is none righteous, no, not one. (Romans 3:10)

> All have sinned and come short of the glory of God. (Romans 3:23)

On the other hand, once someone puts their faith in the Lamb, that His shed blood paid for all of their sins—that every single trespass they have committed has been completely canceled out, then they no longer avoid God. They no longer have a guilty conscience.

> How much more shall the blood of Christ, who through the eternal Spirit offered Himself without spot to God, cleanse your conscience from dead works to serve the living God? (Hebrews 9:14)

> Let us draw near with a sincere heart in full assurance of faith, having our hearts sprinkled clean from an evil conscience and our bodies washed with pure water. (Hebrews 10:22)

Thou hast cast all my sins behind thy back. (Isaiah 38:17)

Come now, let us reason together, says the Lord: though your sins are like scarlet, they shall be as white as snow; though they are red like crimson, they shall become like wool. (Isaiah 1:18)

Who is a God like unto thee ... He will subdue our iniquities; and thou wilt cast all their sins into the depths of the sea. (Micah 7:18-19)

For I will be merciful toward their iniquities, and I will remember their sins no more. (Hebrews 8:12)

I am he who blots out your transgressions for my own sake, and I will not remember your sins. (Isaiah 43:25)

And no longer shall each one teach his neighbor and each his brother, saying, 'Know the Lord,' for they shall all know me, from the least of them to the greatest, declares the Lord. For I will forgive their iniquity, and I will remember their sin no more. (Jeremiah 31:34)

Then he adds, "I will remember their sins and their lawless deeds no more." (Hebrews 10:17)

He is faithful and just to forgive us our sins, and to cleanse us from all unrighteousness. (I John 1:9)

We are now free to come into the presence of the All Powerful, Eternally Just God, and not have to worry about being judged. We are freed from even the consciousness of sin.

Jesus explained to the Pharisees in Matthew 23:23: "You pay tithe of mint and anise and cumin, and have neglected the weightier matters of the law: JUSTICE and MERCY and FAITH. These you ought to have done, without leaving the others undone."

Why are these "weightier matters"?

JUSTICE: God is just and must judge us for our sins;

MERCY: God showed mercy by providing the Lamb to be judged in our place;

FAITH: You must have faith in this Good News for it to benefit you.

◆

YOUR HEART WILL CHANGE FROM REPEL TO ATTRACT

Jesus paid for your sins so you don't have to. When you truly believe this, then your magnet, so to speak, flips around, and instead of being repelled from the Lord you are irresistibly attracted to Him.

This change in behavior from repel to attract was seen in Peter. When he first met Jesus and witnessed Jesus cause a miraculous catch of fish, Peter pleaded "depart from me, for I am a sinful man." (Luke 5:8) But after the resurrection, when Peter witnessed Jesus cause another miraculous catch of fish, he "cast himself into the sea" and swam to Jesus! (John 21:6-7)

When you believe the Gospel, that very instant, you are drawn into the Lord's presence – being one with the Lord – at one moment. You experience the joy of the Lord. You become filled with the Holy Spirit.

> What? know ye not that your body is the temple of the Holy Ghost which is in you, which ye have of God, and ye are not your own? (1 Corinthians 6:19)

> A new heart also will I give you, and a new spirit will I put within you: and I will take away the stony heart out of your flesh ... And I will put my spirit within you, and cause you to walk in my statutes. (Ezekiel 36:26-27)

You experience the Lord's loving presence overwhelming you. You then want to share His love with others.

Unconsciously, your focus begins to shift from self to others.

Instead of spending your time and energy thinking about yourself, trying to get yourself into heaven, you realize that through Christ you are already accepted by God, so you start focusing on others, caring about getting others into heaven!

By the Holy Spirit, people are magnetically

attracted to you, but not actually to you, but to the "Christ in you." (Colossians 1:27)

> As I have loved you, that ye also love one another. By this shall all men know that ye are my disciples, if ye have love one to another. (John 13:34-35)

◆

C.S. LEWIS—THE MOST RELUCTANT CONVERT

At age 19, Clive Staples Lewis fought in the trenches of World War I. After the War, he taught at Magdalen College, Oxford, 1925-54. Then, from 1954-1963, he was the professor of Medieval and Renaissance English at Cambridge University.

He wrote some of the most widely read books in English literature, with over 200 million sold worldwide and, nearly 50 years after his death, still selling a million a year. His notable titles include: *The Problem of Pain*, 1940; *The Screwtape Letters*, 1942; *Abolition of Man*, 1943; *Miracles*, 1947; and *The Chronicles of Narnia*, 1950-1956, which includes the popular work: *The Lion, the Witch and the Wardrobe*.

Originally an agnostic, Lewis wrote of his spiritual journey beginning in 1926, when he met his Catholic colleague at Oxford, J.R.R. Tolkien, the author of *The Hobbit*, 1937, and *Lord of the Rings*, 1937-1949, which is one of the best-selling novels ever written—with over 150 million copies sold.

Lewis wrote in *Surprised by Joy*, 1955, how he resisted believing, "kicking, struggling, resentful, and darting his eyes in every direction for a chance to escape," until finally, in 1929, he was drawn to believe.

A movie was released in 2021 titled *The Most Reluctant Convert—The Untold Story of C.S. Lewis.* He wrote:

> You must picture me alone in that room in Magdalen (College, Oxford) night after night, feeling, whenever my mind lifted even for a second from my work, the steady, unrelenting approach of Him whom I so earnestly desired not to meet ... That which I greatly feared had at last come upon me. In the Trinity Term of 1929 I gave in, and admitted that God was God, and knelt and prayed: perhaps, that night, the most dejected and reluctant convert in all England.

His surrender became complete in 1931, describing an experience after a late-night discussion with J.R.R. Tolkien and Hugo Dyson about faith in Jesus:

> I know very well when, but hardly how, the final step was taken. I was driven to Whipsnade Zoo one sunny morning.

When we set out, I did not believe that Jesus Christ is the Son of God, and when we reached to zoo, I did. Yet I had not exactly spent the journey in thought. Nor in great emotion. 'Emotional' is perhaps the last word we can apply to some of the most important events. It was more like when a man, after long sleep, still lying motionless in bed, becomes aware that he is now awake ... And it was, like that moment on top of the bus, ambiguous.

Freedom, or necessity? Or do they differ at their maximum? At that maximum a man is what he does; there is nothing of him left over or outside the act. As for what we commonly call 'Will,' and what we commonly call 'Emotion,' I fancy these usually talk too loud, protest too much, to be quite believed, and we have a secret suspicion that the great passion or the iron resolution is partly a put-up job ...

They have spoiled Whipsnade since then. Wallaby Wood, with the birds singing overhead and the blue-bells underfoot and the Wallabies hopping all round one, was almost Eden come again.

He wrote:

> Christianity ... is a religion you could not have guessed ... It is not the sort of thing anyone would have made up. It has just that queer twist about it that real things have.

Ronald Reagan described another reluctant convert, February 6, 1984:

> An editor of *TIME* magazine, Whittaker Chambers, in ... (his) autobiography, *Witness* ... marked the beginning of his personal journey away from communism on the day that he was suddenly struck by the sight of his infant daughter's ear as she sat there having breakfast ... He said, he realized that such intricacy, such precision could be no accident, no freak of nature ... He didn't know it at the time, in that moment, God—the finger of God had touched his forehead.

◆

WHAT ABOUT WORKS?

Then they said to Him, "What shall we do, that we may work the works of God?" Jesus answered and said to them, "This is the work of God, that you believe in Him whom He sent." (John 6:28-29; Roman 4:1-8 NKJV)

If believers are not saved by works, but by believing in the sacrifice of the Lamb of God, where do works fit in? The saying is, good works do not precede salvation, but they should follow it. James 2:18 states "I will shew thee my faith by my works." Paul said in Acts 26:20 "I ... shewed ... throughout Judea, and then to the Gentiles, that they should repent and turn to God, and do works meet for repentance."

Hanging apples on an oak tree does not turn it into an apple tree, but a living apple tree should produce apples. Doing good works does not save you – but a person who is saved by faith in Christ should sooner or later produce good works.

It can be the same pile of good works, but the motivation for doing them has changed. Instead of doing works, like Cain, hoping to earn brownie points with God, believers are accepted by God through faith in the blood of Christ, and are filled with the Holy Spirit who does the good works through them to show a lost and dying world the unconditional love of God.

Water may be in a pipe, but which direction is it flowing? Is the person doing works to reach God, or is God doing works through them to reach hurting humanity?

> For it is God who works in you
> to will and to act in order to fulfill his
> good purpose. (Philippians 2:13)

When you believe in the Lamb of God, you are born again, God fills you with the Holy

Spirit who works through you. You are Jesus' hands and feet, sharing the Gospel of God's love with a lost and hurting world.

> For we are his workmanship, created in Christ Jesus unto good works, which God hath before ordained that we should walk in them. (Ephesians 2:10)

Those whose walk with the Lord has become dry, it is because they have kept the living water bottled up. It becomes stale. They are not sharing their faith. The secret to the Christian walk staying fresh is to let the Spirit flow through you in ministry to others. St. Francis of Assisi's Prayer for Peace says:

> O Master, let me not seek as much
> to be consoled as to console,
> to be understood as to understand,
> to be loved as to love.

An example of this was Acts 9:10-19. God ordained that Ananias should lay hands on Paul, and showed Paul a vision of it, but Ananias had to walk it out.

> The Lord called to him in a vision, "Ananias ... Go to the house of Judas on Straight Street and ask for a man from Tarsus named Saul ... In a vision he has seen a man named Ananias come and place his hands on him to restore his sight."

> "Lord," Ananias answered, "I have heard many reports about this

man and all the harm he has done to your holy people" ... But the Lord said to Ananias, "Go! This man is my chosen instrument to proclaim my name to the Gentiles" ...

Then Ananias went to the house and entered it. Placing his hands on Saul, he said, "Brother Saul, the Lord—Jesus, who appeared to you on the road as you were coming here—has sent me so that you may see again and be filled with the Holy Spirit."

Pastor Paul Van Noy of Candlelight Christian Fellowship in Coeur d'Alene, ID, explained:

"Workmanship" in the Greek is the word "poiema," which is derived from "poiima," meaning "poem." Your life is a beautiful poem that God is writing. Good works are the work of God within the believer—in this we shine and God uses us to draw others to Himself.

And when He does the work through you it is not hard.

Take My yoke upon you and learn from Me; for I am gentle and humble in heart, and you will find rest for your souls. For My yoke is easy and My burden is light. (Matthew 11:28-30)

♦

THE TRINITY

To help understanding how God works through believers, it is helpful to study the Trinity. If you look at the prepositions in the New Testament, most of the time a verse refers to God the Father, the prepositions used are *to, unto, of,* and *from,* for example:

> For whosoever shall do the will *of* my Father (Matthew 12:50);

> Come, ye blessed *of* my Father (Matthew 25:34);

> I seek not mine own will, but the will *of* the Father (John 5:30);

> I came forth *from* the Father (John 16:28);

> Pray *to* thy Father which is in secret (Matthew 6:6)

> I leave the world, and go *to* the Father (John 16:28);

> Appear not unto men to fast, but *unto* thy Father (Matthew 6:18);

> Father, *into* thy hands I commend my spirit (Luke 23:46).

Verses that refer to Jesus often use the prepositions *by, through*, and *in,* for example:

> I am the way, the truth and the life; no man cometh unto the Father but *by* me

(John 14:6);

> I am the door: *by* me if any man enter in, he shall be saved (John 10:9);

> But my God shall supply all your need according to his riches in glory *by* Christ Jesus (Philippians 4:19);

> I can do all things *through* Christ which strengtheneth me (Philippians 4:13);

> They taught the people and preached *through* Jesus the resurrection from the dead (Acts. 4:2).

Most of the time a New Testament verse refers to the Holy Spirit the prepositions used are *in* and *with,* for example:

> Comforter, that he may abide *with* you forever (John 14:16);

> Ye shall be baptized *with* the Holy Ghost not many days hence (Acts 1:5);

> And they were all filled *with* the Holy Ghost (Acts 4:31);

> The Spirit of truth; he dwelleth *with* you, and shall be *in* you (John 14:17);

> Walk *in* the Spirit and ye shall not fulfill the lust of the flesh (Galatians 5:16);

> I was *in* the Spirit on the Lord's day (Revelations 1:10).

A humble attempt at explaining this divine relationship is a football game.

God the Father is like the Coach – it is His will that is going to take place on the field. He is in the locker room with the marker board, deciding the plays. But how does His will get onto the field? The Quarterback. He gets the play from the Coach, and wearing a uniform, runs onto the field, being the one player to speak, calling the plays. ("The Word was made flesh and dwelt among us." John 1:14)

Originally, there was only one other player on the field – the Holy Spirit. When the Word was spoken, the Holy Spirit moved over the face of the waters and brought forth life.

Now we are all players on the field, filled with the Holy Spirit, carrying out the will of our Coach, which is communicated to us *in the huddle* by our Quarterback, Jesus!

For all eternity, God the Father, God the Son, and God the Holy Spirit have existed and loved each other completely. Through the Father's plan, we are invited into this divine love relationship, being adopted into Christ, and filled with the Holy Spirit, who loves and glorifies Jesus and the Father through us.

♦

PROMISE OF THE HOLY SPIRIT

Jesus said "I tell you the truth. It is expedient for you that I go away: for if I go not away, the Comforter will not come unto you; but if I depart, I will send Him unto you ... When the Spirit of truth is come, He will guide you into all truth." (John 16:7, 13-14)

The Holy Spirit works the Father's will in us and helps us to overcome difficulties.

> Remember the word that I said to you ... If they persecuted Me, they will also persecute you ... But when the Helper comes, whom I shall send to you from the Father, the Spirit of truth who proceeds from the Father, He will testify of Me. And you also will bear witness. (John 15:20-27)

> And I will ask the Father, and He will give you another Helper, that He may be with you forever; (John 14:16)

> He who believes in Me, the works that I do he will do also; and greater works than these he will do, because I go to My Father. (John 14:12)

> But the Helper, the Holy Spirit, whom the Father will send in My name, He will teach you all things, and bring to your remembrance all that I said to you. (John 14:26 NASB)

> After listening to the message of truth, the Gospel of your salvation – having also believed, you were sealed in Him with the Holy Spirit of promise, who is given as a pledge of our inheritance. (Ephesians 1:13-14)

♦

THE HOLY SPIRIT AND YOUR HEART

Every day you make choices of what to think, say and do. You make plans, you budget, you organize, you have a vision for your life and take steps to achieve it. In the framework of innumerable things that you have absolutely no control over you have a small basket of things that you can control. And you have a choice: pursuing your plans or God's plans?

The Holy Spirit is called the Paraclete, or Helper. The Holy Spirit helps you to make the right choices by gently prompting your conscience, "in the still small voice," to act in accordance with the Father's will. For there to be unity in Heaven there can only be one will – the Father's. Two or more wills would bring division.

Have you ever tuned a guitar string to a piano? Out of key, there is a dissonance, a harsh, disagreeable sound. But when it comes into tune, there is a resonance of vibrations, a beautiful unity. When your will is out of tune with your Creator's will, there is dissonance, a continual unsettledness in your heart. When you submit your will to His, there is resonance, an indescribable peace deep within your soul.

Since God is perfect and does not change, anything the Holy Spirit leads you to do will always be in line with God's word, it will be in line with what the Holy Spirit has spoken in the past, as revealed in the Holy Scriptures. That is why it is important to develop the habit of daily Bible reading.

I John 4:1-6 says to "test the spirits," that is, compare everything someone is telling you, and every thought that comes into your mind, with God's word.

Every thought you choose to entertain and act upon, reveals your heart, your choice of wanting to do your will or God's will.

> The Lord searches all hearts and understands every plan and thought. (I Chronicles 28:9)

> I the LORD search the heart. (Jeremiah 17:10)

> For man looketh on the outward appearance, but the Lord looketh on the heart. (I Samuel 16:7)

> The Lord knoweth the thoughts of man. (Psalm 94:11)

> The word of God ... is a discerner of the thoughts and intents of the heart. (Hebrews 4:12)

God created man and woman, and expectantly hoped for a close relationship with them. He wanted to be the desire of their hearts and included in their thoughts. In Genesis 6, before Noah's flood, is one of the saddest verses in the Bible:

> And God saw that the wickedness of man was great in the earth, and that every imagination of the thoughts of his heart was only evil continually. And it repented the Lord that he had made man on the earth, and it grieved him at his heart.

The Living Bible says: "It broke his heart"; God's Word Translation says: "He was heartbroken." Then next verse stated:

> And the Lord said, I will destroy man whom I have created from the face of the earth ... for it repenteth me that I have made them.

> Roman 1:28 "And even as they did not like to retain God in their knowledge, God gave them over to a debased mind."

> Zephaniah 1:6 "And them that are turned back from the Lord; and those that have not sought the Lord, nor enquired for him."

> Psalm 10:4 "The wicked ... will not seek after God: God is not in all his thoughts."

Thankfully, Genesis 6:8 recorded "But Noah found grace in the eyes of the Lord."

> A book of remembrance was

written before him for them that feared the Lord, and that thought upon his name. And they shall be mine, saith the Lord. (Malachi 3:16-18)

♦

GOD IS OUTSIDE OF TIME–WE LIVE IN SLOW MOTION

If God gives people the ability and opportunity to love and worship Him, it also means they could potentially make the choice to reject Him — yet He still works His will in all creation. Let's examine this.

In 1997, a computer named Deep Blue defeated the world chess champion Garry Kasparov. In 2017, Google's AlphaGo computer defeated Ke Jie, China's champion of the complicated strategy game called "go."

Computers used AI –Artificial Intelligence, to calculate every possible move that could be made, and then predict what each player would do.

The desire to predict outcomes on an ever-larger scale has led to a "quantum supremacy" race to build the fastest supercomputers. Each year news reports announce faster ones being developed, led by U.S., Japan, China, Russia, France, Italy, Switzerland, Finland, Taiwan, Saudi Arabia, and the United Arab Emirates.

Instead of conventional computers which use "bits" of digital information, supercomputers use quantum bits, or qubits, which can exist in many states simultaneously. The more qubits that are "entangled" the more the processing speed increases exponentially.

Speed is measured in petaFLOPS, or PFLOPS –one quadrillion floating-point operations per second; and Exaflops– one quintillion floating point operations per second. That is a billion billion, or 1,000,000,000,000,000,000 operations per second. As of May 31, 2022, Oak Ridge National Laboratory's Frontier supercomputer performed 1.102 Exaflops (10^{18}) per second.

IBM is working on a 1,121-qubit quantum computing chip called Condor, scheduled for release in 2024, and a 4,000-qubit chip by 2025. Intel is working on a silicon qubit chip, or silicon quantum dot, for a million-qubit quantum computer, with each silicon qubit operating as a single electron transistor, manipulated using radio frequency pulses at the specific resonant frequency of each qubit.

China has a prototype light-based photon quantum computer, Jiuzhang 2.0, designed to be one septillion times faster than the world's fastest existing supercomputer. According to Xinhua News Agency, it will be able to calculate in one millisecond a task that would take the world's fastest conventional computer 30 trillion years.

Supercomputers are cryogenically cooled to near absolute zero, as any warmer the qubits experience thermal noise, vibrate, and lose their coherence. Scientists in Australia are working on embedding qubits in synthetic diamonds to run at room temperature.

Super computers use AI to perform complex algorithms to analyze enormous amounts of constantly changing complicated variables in order to make predictions.

Dr. Darío Gil, IBM Senior Vice President and Director of Research stated: "Quantum computing has the power to transform nearly every sector and help us tackle the biggest problems of our time."

Uses include simulating nuclear explosions, tsunamis, earthquakes, climate change, weather patterns, oil exploration; recreating the condition in the first few seconds after the Big Bang; creating 3D maps of the universe, the human brain, the human genome; tracking spread of infectious diseases; creating molecules to fight COVID; and forecasting large-scale human behavior. The overriding purpose of supercomputers is predictive.

If humans can make computers this fast in an attempt to predict the world's future, do you think God is faster? Yes! Absolutely! He is faster than infinity times infinity computations per second. Compared to God, we are living in slow motion. He is so far beyond fast that He is outside of time, existing in an ever-present now! To Him, time stands still. As mentioned earlier, II Peter 3:8 says, "A day is with the Lord as a thousand years."

We make our choices, but He can adjust every atom in the universe to insure His will takes place on Earth.

♦

GOD KNOWS ALL POSSIBLE FUTURES

Charles Dickens's *A Christmas Carol*, 1843, culminates in the scene:

> The Spirit stood among the graves, and pointed down to one ... "Before I draw nearer to that stone to which you point," said Scrooge, "answer me one question. Are these the shadows of the things that Will be, or are they shadows of things that May be" ... Still the Ghost pointed downward to the grave ...
>
> "Men's courses will foreshadow certain ends, to which, if persevered in, they must lead," said Scrooge. "But if the courses be departed from, the ends will change. Say it i thus with what you show me" ...
>
> "Spirit." he cried, tight clutching at its robe, "hear me. I am not the man I was. I will not be the man I must have been ... Why show me this, if I am past all hope" ...
>
> The hand appeared to shake. "Good Spirit," he pursued, as down upon the ground he fell ... "Assure me that I yet may change these shadows you have shown me, by an altered life."

God not only knows the future, He knows all *possible futures* and tells us what they are. He even tells us how we should choose, and in His infinite wisdom, He knows how we will choose. "There is no limit to what he knows" (Psalm 147:5)

God put the Tree in the Garden of Eden and told Adam and Eve: "Thou shalt not eat of it: for in the day that thou eatest thereof thou shalt surely die." (Genesis 2:16-17).

God told Cain: "IF thou doest well, shalt thou not be accepted? and IF thou doest not well, sin lieth at the door." (Genesis 4:7)

God gave the Children of Israel the Law and told them what their future would be IF they followed it and IF they DID NOT.

Deuteronomy 28: "IF thou shalt HEARKEN diligently unto the voice of the Lord thy God, to observe and to do all his commandments ... the Lord thy God will set thee on high above all nations of the earth: And all these BLESSINGS SHALL COME ON THEE, AND OVERTAKE THEE ... But it shall come to pass, IF thou wilt NOT HEARKEN unto the voice of the Lord thy God, to observe to do all his commandments ... that all these CURSES SHALL COME UPON THEE, AND OVERTAKE THEE."

God even told them how to choose:

> I have set before you LIFE and DEATH, BLESSINGS and CURSES. Now CHOOSE LIFE, so that you and your children may live. (Deuteronomy 30:19)

The word "IF" occurs some 1,600 times in the Bible, such as when Abraham sent his servant to get a wife for his son:

> And IF the woman will not be willing to follow thee, THEN thou shalt be clear from this my oath: only bring not my son thither again. (Genesis 24:8)

Jeremiah 18:7-10 forewarned:

> I went down to the potter's house, and there he was, making something at the wheel. And the vessel that he made of clay was marred in the hand of the potter; so he made it again into another vessel, as it seemed good to the potter to make ...
>
> O house of Israel, can I not do with you as this potter? says the Lord. Look, as the clay is in the potter's hand, so are you in My hand, O house of Israel! ... At any time I might announce that a nation or kingdom will be uprooted, torn down, and destroyed. But IF that nation I warned turns from its evil, THEN I will relent of the disaster I had planned to bring.
>
> And IF at another time I announce that I will build up and establish a nation or kingdom, and IF it does evil in My sight and does not listen to My voice, THEN I will relent of the good I had intended for it.

Jeremiah 17:24-27 stated:

> It shall come to pass, IF ye diligently hearken unto me, saith the Lord, to ... hallow the sabbath day, to do no work therein; THEN ... this city shall remain for ever ... But IF ye will not hearken unto me to hallow the sabbath day ... THEN will I kindle a fire in the gates thereof, and it shall devour the palaces of Jerusalem, and it shall not be quenched.

Similarly, Jeremiah 38:17-18 recorded:

> Jeremiah said to Zedekiah ... The God of Israel says: IF you indeed surrender to the officers of the king of Babylon, THEN you will live, this city will not be burned down, and you and your household will survive. But IF you do not surrender to the officers of the king of Babylon, THEN this city will be delivered into the hands of the Chaldeans. They will burn it down, and you yourself will not escape their grasp.

II Chronicles 7:14 states:

> IF my people, which are called by my name, shall humble themselves, and pray, and seek my face, and turn from their wicked ways; THEN will I hear from heaven, and will forgive their sin, and will heal their land.

Almost half of the 574 New Testament occurrences of the word "IF" are by Jesus, who always presents it on man's side and never on God's side.

> Matthew 6:14-15 For IF you forgive men their trespasses, your heavenly Father will also forgive you. But IF you do not forgive men their trespasses, neither will your Father forgive your trespasses.

If God wants you to do something on earth, you can yield in faith and He can bring forth through you a harvest "some thirty-fold, some sixty, and some a hundred" (Mark 4:20); "that ye may prove what is that good, and acceptable, and perfect will of God." (Romans 12:2)

One more example. In First Samuel 23, God showed David what the potential future would be, thus allowing him to choose a different one. David and his men were in the city of Keilah when they were told King Saul was considering coming there to capture them:

> David said to Abiathar the priest, Bring hither the ephod. Then said David, "O LORD ... will Saul come down, as thy servant hath heard?" ... And the LORD said, "He will come down." Then said David, "Will the men of Keilah deliver me and my men into the hand of Saul?" And the LORD said, "They will deliver thee up."

Then David and his men, which were about six hundred, arose and departed out of Keilah ... And it was told Saul that David was escaped from Keilah; and he gave up going there.

The future holds an ocean of possibilities, the shore is where the future meets the present, but once a decision is made it is past, immovable as land.

♦

AI—ARTIFICIAL INTELLIGENCE

Allegories are imperfect, but helpful. A lot of attention is given to AI — Artificial Intelligence. On June 13, 2022, it was reported that Google has an AI computer named LaMDA which reportedly has "sentience" or self-awareness. Imagine if you could create an A.I. robot that could think, learn, talk, and make choices. Maybe you make a number of them, but shockingly, the best one comes up with a plot to kill you and gets a third of the others to join in. What do you do? Perhaps lock them up!

But you still want to create, so this time you make AI beings with limited functionality. You put them in a virtual world, maybe inside a big warehouse, and hardwire all of them to shut off in ten years. Sometime within those ten years each one will be presented with the choice of joining a plot to kill you, or out of love for you be willing to suffer rejection, even voluntarily shutting themselves off before they would ever do anything against you.

After ten years, they are all shut off. Question: which ones would you like to reactivate? To resurrect? Obviously, the ones who love you so much they would rather shut themselves off before they would ever do anything against you. Now you can reactivate them, remove the ten-year limitation and give them full functionality. You can let them out of the virtual warehouse and enjoy being with them without having to worry about any of them plotting behind your back to kill you, because they were each presented with that choice and decided they loved you more than their own lives. What do you do with the rest of them? Maybe melt them down!

> Blessed and holy is he that hath part of the first resurrection: on such the second death has no power. (Revelation 20:5-6)

Are we, in a sense, "artificial intelligence"? In other words, God, who has existed for eternity, is omniscient, all-knowing, all-intelligent. There is no intelligence outside of Him. If any created beings have intelligence, it is because He gave it to them. God's plan is to populate heaven with beings made in His image who want to be with Him. He can enjoy being with us forever and not have to be concerned about anyone plotting behind His back, as Satan did. Everyone there will have already faced that choice and will have chosen to do God's will above their own!

◆

SPIRIT—MIND—BODY

You are a spirit, you possess a mind, and you live in a body. Your spirit is drawn toward God, your body is drawn away from God, and your mind is in the middle, like a switch, deciding who wins — spirit or body. The battle is for your mind.

Your mind is like a super fancy computer. It is a lot more than that, but it is at least that. And your body is like the computer case, which makes it silly for people to argue over what color it is — "blue computers are better than green computers!?" It does not matter what color the case of a computer or cell phone is.

What matters is the software, the apps, are running on it! It does not matter what color someone's skin is, what matters is what "behavioral software" is running on their brain! Is it "love your enemies," "forgive and you will be forgiven," "do unto others as you would have them do unto you"; or is it selfishness, hard-heartedness, cancel your enemies, make them pay, retaliate!

The battle is over what thinking is going on in your mind, whose software gets loaded on your brain — God's Word, or Satan's corrupted files, malware, and viruses.

When God made Adam and Eve, they had the factory settings on their brains' software, an innocence that allowed them to hear God's voice. God gave them free will, and it was as if He then said, —Oh, one last thing, don't open email from someone you don't know and download the attachment.

Eve gets an email with the subject line, —You just won a million dollars, click here to download. She was deceived and downloaded the virus of selfishness.

Viruses send themselves to other computers. There was only one other computer in the garden, Adam's. Adam knew he was disobeying God, but he downloaded the attachment anyway. Then the virus got into Cain, who selfishly killed Abel. It mutated and got into all creation, with animals killing each other. "For we know that the whole creation groaneth and travaileth in pain together until now." (Romans 8:22)

Then God sent a software fix, a patch, called the Law. The Levite priests were the computer techs who "line by line, precept by precept," corrected each line of code in the corrupted behavioral software. "He restoreth my soul." (Psalm 23:3)

Finally, God promised to send software version 2.0, and burn it on their hard drives. Jeremiah 31:33 "'But this is the new covenant I will make with the people of Israel after those days,' says the LORD. 'I will put my instructions deep within them, and I will write them on their hearts.'"

Peter and the Apostles got the New Version downloaded into them from the "Cloud" on the day of Pentecost. Their behavior changed from cowardly denying Christ to boldly proclaiming Him. They had a new operating system.

Have you ever downloaded software and then see the message that you have to restart in order for the update to go into effect? In the same way, it is one thing hearing the Good News of the Gospel, but it does not go into effect until you reboot, until you have a rebirth. You have to first shut down, die to your selfish will, be willing to give up your own plans, surrender your life, and then the Lord restarts you! You are born again, living with a new operating system.

Then there is memory backup.

Your computer or cell phone stores memory on it, but those memory files are also backed up in real time to a cloud server, such as iCloud, DropBox, iTunes, or Google Cloud. In a similar way, your computer brain records every thought you think and every word you speak, but your memory files are also backed up in real time to God's iCloud. "For by your words you will be justified, and by your words you will be condemned."

If your computer crashes or your cell phone breaks, you can get a new, better one and simply download your memory files from the cloud server onto it. Similarly, someday your computer case body will break, your hard drive will crash – you will die. At the Resurrection, you will be given an amazing eternal body, like Jesus' when He rose from the dead, and you will be given a brand new, lightning-fast brain.

But you would not be you without your memory files. You would just be a beautiful body with a blank super-fast brain, so God will download all your memory files into your new brain — without the sinful memories, of course, which He will scrub away by His blood. In heaven, you will be able to recognize and remember people, places, decisions, similar to Jesus after His Resurrection when He walked into the room and knew all His disciples.

♦

PREDESTINATION AND FREE WILL

One of the most studied questions in physics is whether light is a particle or a wave. One of the most studied theological questions is whether God predetermined who He will or will not give grace to, or if He sends grace to everyone in hopes men and women will respond and repent — fully knowing in advance who will respond to His grace and who will resist it.

Is it possible to somehow hold both views? Astrophysicist Dr. Ross spoke at Mosaic Christian Church, January 30, 2020:

> I spend a lot of time in my book, *Beyond the Cosmos,* showing ways you

can resolve divine predestination and human free will.

Christianity teaches that there is a God that is beyond space and time that has predetermined every thought you will think, every word you will speak, and every action you will perform before He created the universe.

But it also teaches that He is holding you responsible for every thought you think, every word you speak, and action you perform—He has given you the freedom to choose what you are going to think, speak and do. The Bible teaches both.

Now, from our limited dimensional perspective, this looks like an utter contradiction. How can God control everything and yet claim that we are in control of our thoughts, words and actions ...

Other religions teach either that God predetermines everything, which is what you see in Islam, for example; or as you see in Eastern Religions that God does not predetermine anything, that it is all human free will. The Bible stands alone in teaching both.

In fact, I put into my book, *Beyond*

the Cosmos, all the passages in the Bible that teach that we human beings have free will, the freedom to choose what we think, say and do. And there are over 1,500 passages ...

But likewise, there are virtually an equal number of passages that says that God controls everything, that everything is predetermined from before the creation of the universe. And there are eight verses in the Bible that teach both doctrines in the same sentence.

You really cannot avoid the idea that the Bible teaches both. Many Christians have tried to look at the Bible in such a way that they claim it is predestination and not free will; or human free will and not predestination. But if you actually do a thorough Bible study it teaches both, claiming that both simultaneously operate ...

It is not a contradiction. It is a resolvable paradox if we allow God to be as powerful as He is.

Dr. Ross said in *Beyond the Cosmos* (2017):

From the divine perspective, God calls or chooses those who will be saved; while from our human perspective we do the calling or choosing.

God shared His plan for Abraham's seed:

And he said unto Abram, Know of a surety that thy seed shall be a stranger in a land that is not theirs, and shall serve them; and they shall afflict them four hundred years; And also that nation, whom they shall serve, will I judge: and afterward shall they come out with great substance ... But in the fourth generation they shall come hither again: for the iniquity of the Amorites is not yet full. (Genesis 15:13-16)

Paul acknowledged that God had "separated" him, yet Paul had to make the decision to do something—preach:

But when it pleased God, who separated me from my mother's womb, and called me by his grace, to reveal his Son in me, that I might preach him among the heathen. (Galatians 1:15-16)

God "put into the heart of Titus" a concern for the saints, yet it was Titus who actually made the decision to go to them "on his own initiative":

Thanks be to God, who put into the heart of Titus the same concern I have for you. For Titus not only welcomed our appeal, but he is coming to you with much enthusiasm and on his own initiative. (II Corinthians 8:16-17)

"Delight yourself in the Lord and He will give you the desires of your heart." (Psalm 37:4) One way of reading this is, if you delight yourself in the Lord, you will be praying "Thy will be done." (Luke 11:2). He will put into your heart the desire to do His will — you will want to do what He wants Then He will give you the faith to believe for it.

David said in Psalm 63:

> You are my God. I worship you. In my heart, I long for you ... Your love means more than life to me ... I think about you, God, before I go to sleep, and my thoughts turn to you during the night.

There are verses indicating that it is God who puts a thought or desire into someone's heart, but it is up to them to decide to act it out:

> I had not told anyone what my God had put in my heart to do for Jerusalem. (Nehemiah 2:11)

> Then my God put it into my heart to assemble the nobles, the officials, and the other people to be enrolled by genealogies. (Nehemiah 7:5)

> The LORD moved the heart of Cyrus king of Persia to make a proclamation throughout his realm. (Ezra 1:1)

> Praise be to the LORD ... who has put it into the king's heart to bring honor to the house of the LORD in Jerusalem

in this way. (Ezra 7:27)

> Now all the earth sought the presence of Solomon to hear his wisdom, which God had put in his heart. (I Kings 10:24)

> For God has put it into their hearts to fulfill His purpose. (Revelation 17:17)

> Now may the Lord direct your hearts into the love of God. (2 Thessalonians 3:5)

> I know, O LORD, that a man's way is not his own; no one who walks directs his own steps. (Jeremiah 10:23)

Will you invite the Lord to stir up your heart to worship Him? Exodus 35:21 described:

> And they came, every one whose heart stirred him up, and every one whom his spirit made willing, and they brought the Lord's offering to the work of the tabernacle.

It is impossible to comprehend how these two biblical doctrines can both exist, yet they are both necessary in our relationship with God:

> 1) that He is in complete control of everything in the universe; and

> 2) that you exercise free will in living your day-to-day life.

To be able to have faith, you must rest and "be still," trusting that God is in complete control, that He is all-powerful, that before you were created He had a plan for your life, that He opens and closes doors, and that He has prepared an eternal future of blessings for you. David wrote: "You are my God. My times are in your hand." (Psalm 31:14) Jesus said, "Times or seasons that the Father has fixed by his own authority." (Acts 1:7)

On the other hand, in your everyday life, you must actively seek God's will, pray that His will be done through you, and do things, including being open to His leading to share the Gospel with others so that they too may be saved. Ben Franklin wrote:

> Work as if you were to live a hundred years. Pray as if you were to die tomorrow.

Connecticut Governor Jonathan Trumbull wrote to Washington during the Revolution:

> In this day of calamity, to trust altogether to the justice of our cause, without our utmost exertion, would be tempting Providence ... Play the man for God, and for the cities of our God. (2 Samuel 10:12)

C.S. Lewis put in *The Great Divorce*, 1946:

> Ye cannot fully understand the relations of choice and Time till you are beyond both ... What concerns you is the nature of the choice itself ...
>
> Time is the very lens through

which ye see ... as men see through the wrong end of a telescope — something that would otherwise be too big for ye to see at all ... It is a picture of moments following one another and yourself in each moment making some choice that might have been otherwise ...

Every attempt to see the shape of eternity except through the lens of Time destroys your knowledge of freedom.

C.S. Lewis wrote:

Relying on God has to begin all over again every day as if nothing had yet been done.

An example of perspectives is Isaac Newton's First Law of Motion, that every object in nature exists either at rest or in motion:

An object at rest will remain at rest unless an unbalanced force acts upon it, and an object in motion tends to stay in motion unless an external force acts upon it.

But from the larger perspective of relativity, if an object is on the Earth, even if it is at rest, it is still moving as the Earth rotates at 1,000 miles an hour near the equator, in addition to orbiting the Sun at 66,660 miles per hour, in addition to our solar system flying around the center of the Milky Way Galaxy at 536,865 mph.

♦

PROPHECIES FULFILLED

One of the ways God reveals that He is in complete control of everything is through prophecies being made and then fulfilled. One third of the Bible is made up of prophecies. In the Old Testament, there are over 350 prophecies about the Messiah which Jesus fulfilled through his birth, life, death and resurrection, such as:

He would be born in Bethlehem. (Micah 5:2)

He would be born of a virgin. (Isaiah 7:14)

He would be a descendant of David (Isaiah 9:7)

He would be betrayed for 30 pieces of silver. (Zechariah 11:12)

He would be mocked. (Psalm 22:7,8)

He would be crucified. (John 3:14)

He would be pierced. (Psalms 22:16)

He would die with the wicked yet be buried with the rich. (Isaiah 53:9)

That one person, by random chance, could fulfill just eight prophecies is considered a statistical impossibility. Josh and Sean McDowell's book *Evidence That Demands a Verdict* (2017), quotes Professor Peter W. Stoner, Chairman of the Departments of Mathematics and Astronomy at Pasadena City College, who stated:

We find that the chance that

any man might have lived down to the present time and fulfilled all eight prophecies is 1 in 10^{17} (1 in 100,000,000,000,000,000).

Fulfilled prophecies are proof of Jesus' divinity! Robert Morris Page (1903-1992) was the physicist who invented pulsation radar used for the detection of aircraft. He held 37 patents; served with the Naval Research Laboratory in Washington, D.C., received the U.S. Navy Distinguished Civilian Service Award, and the Presidential Certificate of Merit. Robert Morris Page, the son of a Methodist minister, stated of the over 300 Old Testament prophecies fulfilled by Jesus:

> The authenticity of the writings of the prophets, though the men themselves are human, is established by such things as the prediction of highly significant events far in the future that could be accomplished only through a knowledge obtained from a realm which is not subject to the laws of time as we know them.
>
> One of the great evidences is the long series of prophecies concerning Jesus the Messiah. These prophecies extend hundreds of years prior to the birth of Christ. They include a vast amount of detail concerning Christ himself, His nature and the things

He would do when He came—things which to the natural world, or the scientific world, remain to this day completely inexplicable.

The brilliance of prophecies is that they had to be vague enough so Satan could not figure them out and stop them; but clear enough, so that after Jesus rose from the dead, they would confirm He was the Promised Messiah.

The first prophecy was Genesis 3:15, where God told the serpent Satan, "And I will put enmity between you and the woman, and between your seed and her Seed; He shall bruise your head, and you shall bruise His heel."

C.S. Lewis wrote in *Mere Christianity*, 1952:

The Eternal Being, who knows everything and who created the whole universe, became not only a man but (before that) a baby, and before that a fetus in a woman's body.

Satan is not all-knowing. He did not know when or how this would happen, but he wanted to stop it. This was demonstrated when King Herod was visited by the Magi, the Wise Men from the east. When they asked to see the newborn King of the Jews, Herod flew into a panic and:

... called together all the people's chief priests and teachers of the law, he asked them where the Messiah was to be born. "In Bethlehem in

Judea," they replied, "for this is what the prophet has written" ...

> When Herod realized that he had been outwitted by the Magi, he was furious, and he gave orders to kill all the boys in Bethlehem and its vicinity who were two years old and under. (Matthew 2:4-16)

Had Satan, as was seen operating through evil Herod, been able to understand prophecies, he would have tried to stop every one of them throughout the centuries from coming to pass, but he could not, as they were written in such a way that they were a mystery to him.

> But we speak the wisdom of God in a mystery, even the hidden wisdom, which God ordained before the world unto our glory:

> Which none of the princes of this world knew: for had they known it, they would not have crucified the Lord of glory. (1 Corinthians 2:7-8)

But after the resurrection, the prophecies confirmed Jesus as Savior. He walked with disciples along the road to Emmaus, "and beginning at Moses and all the Prophets, He expounded to them in all the Scriptures the things concerning Himself." (Luke 24:27)

This is like looking at a corn field from one angle and it seems completely random, but turn the corner and look at it from another angle and you see neat-ordered rows.

It is like the Cracker Jack box prize of a lenticular picture — a small card with a vertically ribbed plastic surface, where the image changes with the viewing angle. Prophecies from the angle Satan sees them are indiscernible; but from the angle revealed to the believer by the Holy Spirit, they are clear.

Paul wrote:

> The mystery of Christ, which in other ages was not made known unto the sons of men, as it is now revealed unto his holy apostles and prophets by the Spirit. (Ephesians 3:1-5)

> The preaching of Jesus Christ, according to the revelation of the mystery, which was kept secret since the world began, But now is made manifest, and by the scriptures of the prophets ... made known to all nations for the obedience of faith. (Romans 16:25-27)

> The mystery, which from the beginning of the world hath been hid in God, who created all things by Jesus Christ: To the intent that now unto the principalities and powers in heavenly places might be known by the church. (Ephesians 3:9-12)

The mystery which hath been hid from ages and from generations, but now is made manifest to his saints ... which is Christ in you, the hope of glory. (Colossians 1:26-27)

C.S. Lewis said in *Mere Christianity, 1952:*

I am trying here to prevent anyone saying the really foolish thing that people often say about Him: "I'm ready to accept Jesus as a great moral teacher, but I don't accept his claim to be God." That is the one thing we must not say.

A man who was merely a man and said the sort of things Jesus said would not be a great moral teacher. He would either be a lunatic – on the level with the man who says he is a poached egg – or else he would be the Devil of Hell ... You must make your choice.

Either this man was, and is, the Son of God, or else a madman or something worse. You can shut him up for a fool, you can spit at him and kill him as a demon or you can fall at his feet and call him Lord and God, but let us not come with any patronizing nonsense about his being a great human teacher. He has not left that open to us. He did not intend to.

John 19:30 states that at the crucifixion:

> When Jesus therefore had received the vinegar, he said, It is finished: and he bowed his head, and gave up the ghost.

Satan must have wondered, —what was finished? He thought he had won. He got the Jews and Gentle Romans to crucify Christ. But he lost, as the Lamb of God was sacrificed for the sins of the world so that both Jews and Gentiles would have the opportunity to be accepted by God through faith in Christ. Satan bruised Jesus' heel, but he got his head crushed.

Then Jesus rose from the dead to prove He was who He said He was.

> Great is the mystery of godliness: God was manifest in the flesh, justified in the Spirit, seen of angels, preached unto the Gentiles, believed on in the world, received up into glory. (1Timothy 3:16)

♦

YIELDING TO GOD'S GRACE

How can God's grace acting on one's free will be described? An attempt at is this—have you ever met someone who, when they walk in, their presence fills the room? Well, imagine that times infinity. God's grace is, in essence, His presence. When He allows His presence to manifest, it is like the warmth of the sun which melts your heart like butter.

On the other hand, if He hides His presence, you are left to your own heart and your own thoughts. You focus is on yourself. Your heart grows selfish, cold and hardened. Jeremiah 33:5 "I have hidden my face from this city because of all their evil." C.S. Lewis wrote:

> Everyone says forgiveness is a lovely idea, until they have something to forgive.

Have you ever held a grudge—willfully hardening your heart towards someone who has wronged you? That is essentially how it feels when someone hardens their heart to the Holy Spirit. But when you experience the loving presence of the Holy Spirit, your heart softens, you release the hurt, and forgive them.

Some have stubbornly resisted the Holy Spirit, grieving Him. They choose to harbor grudges, which gradually deadens their consciences. Though it is difficult to understand, Paul asked in Romans 9:19 "For who hath resisted his will?" Stephen, the first martyr, confronted the Sanhedrin:

> Ye stiff-necked and uncircumcised in heart and ears, ye do always resist the Holy Ghost: as your fathers did, so do ye. (Acts 7:51)

> Psalm 95:10 stated: "For forty years I was grieved with that generation, And said, 'It is a people who go astray

in their hearts, And they do not know My ways.'" (re: Hebrews 3:10, 17)

How often they provoked Him in the wilderness, And grieved Him in the desert! Yes, again and again they tempted God, And limited the Holy One of Israel. They did not remember His power: The day when He redeemed them from the enemy. (Psalm 78:40-42)

Yea, they made their hearts as an adamant stone, lest they should hear the law, and the words which the LORD of hosts hath sent in his Spirit by the former prophets. (Zechariah 7:12-13)

Paul wrote in Ephesians 4:30-32:

And do not grieve the Holy Spirit of God, with whom you were sealed for the day of redemption. Get rid of all bitterness, rage and anger, brawling and slander, along with every form of malice.

Be kind and compassionate to one another, forgiving each other, just as in Christ God forgave you.

Paul warned not to be as those who "withstood" with "their conscience seared":

In the last days perilous times shall come. For men shall be lovers of their own selves, covetous, boasters, proud ... as Jannes and Jambres withstood Moses, so do these also resist the truth. (2 Timothy 3;1-8)

Now the Spirit speaketh expressly, that in the latter times some shall depart from the faith, giving heed to seducing spirits ... having their conscience seared with a hot iron. (1Timothy 4:1-2)

Before receiving communion, believers are admonished to forgive, to keep their hearts soft. Jesus stated in the Sermon on the Mount:

Leave your gift there before the altar ... be reconciled to your brother, and then come and offer your gift. (Matthew 5:24)

In a parable, Jesus cautioned:

The master summoned him and declared, 'You wicked servant! I forgave all your debt because you begged me. Shouldn't you have had mercy on your fellow servant ...

In anger his master turned him over to the jailers ... That is how My heavenly Father will treat each of you unless you forgive your brother from your heart. (Matthew 18: 32-35)

Jesus taught the disciples to pray "forgive us our trespasses as we forgive those who trespass against us."

♦

HIS WILL BE DONE—THROUGH EACH OF US

Daniel read in the Book of Jeremiah 25:11-12: 29:3, that the Jewish captivity was to end after seventy years, so he set himself to pray for God's will to be done. God sovereignly raised up King Cyrus to free the Jews to rebuild the Temple "For Jacob my servant's sake, and Israel mine elect, I have even called thee by name ... though thou hast not known me." (Isaiah 45:4)

God graciously gives us the opportunity to participate with Him—to willfully let Him use us to carry out His will. Yet, if you refuse, He will raise up someone else to carry out His will, as in the Book of Esther 4:14, Mordecai told Queen Esther:

> For if you remain silent at this time ... deliverance will arise for the Jews from another place, but you and your father's house will perish. Yet who knows whether you have come to the kingdom for such a time as this?

When we pray the line in the "Our Father" prayer — "Thy kingdom come, Thy will be done, on Earth as it is in Heaven"—it includes an implicit prayer for His will to be done IN and THROUGH us. You are praying, here I am, Lord, where do you need me? We are inviting and giving Him permission to use us as instruments to manifest His will on Earth:

> Present yourselves to God as those
> who have been brought from death to life,
> and your members to God as instruments
> for righteousness. (Romans 6:12-13)

The Lord could have healed Paul's blindness Himself, but instead He told Annanias to go and lay hands on Paul for him to regain his sight. (Acts 9:10-18) He could have appeared to Cornelius, but instead He sent an angel to tell him to send for Peter, and gave Peter a vision telling him to preach to Cornelius. (Acts 10)

Many have experienced unexplainable providential encounters which reaffirm the Lord's divine hand in directing their lives. Some call these divinely timed coincidences "God-incidences," or "God moments."

At the Constitutional Convention, Ben Franklin called these "instances of a superintending providence," June 28, 1787:

> In the beginning of the contest with Great Britain, when we were sensible of danger, we had daily prayer in this room for divine protection. Our prayers, Sir, were heard and they were graciously answered. All of us who were engaged in the struggle must have observed frequent instances of a superintending providence in our favor.

When someone does a good act, it reverberates in a domino effect for good. Likewise, when someone does a selfish act, it reverberates for evil.

Why is there evil in the world? When Adam sinned, it opened the door for evil to come into the world. When people insist on their own selfish ways, there are repercussions of terrible injustices. If God were to stop people from choosing evil, He would also be stopping them from choosing good, and we would be like robots with no free will. When people do unjust acts, a just God has to judge them unless they repent. He may postpone judgment if believers intercede in prayer.

When the Israelites refused to enter the Promised Land, God told Moses "I will smite them with the pestilence, and disinherit them, and will make of thee a greater nation," but after Moses interceded "The Lord said, I have pardoned according to thy word" (Numbers 14). When they sinned with the golden calf, Exodus 32 recorded:

> The Lord said to Moses, "I have seen this people, and indeed it is a stiff-necked people! Now therefore, let Me alone, that My wrath may burn hot against them and I may consume them. And I will make of you a great nation." Then Moses pleaded with the Lord his God, and ... the Lord relented from the harm which He said He would do to His people.

When Israel was on a sinful trajectory for judgment, the Prophet Amos interceded:

This is what the Sovereign Lord showed me: He was preparing swarms of locusts ... as the late crops were coming up. When they had stripped the land clean, I cried out, "Sovereign Lord, forgive! How can Jacob survive? He is so small!" So the Lord relented. "This will not happen," the Lord said.

This is what the Sovereign Lord showed me: The Sovereign Lord was calling for judgment by fire; it dried up the great deep and devoured the land. Then I cried out, "Sovereign Lord, I beg you, stop! How can Jacob survive? He is so small!" So the Lord relented. "This will not happen either," the Sovereign Lord said.

The Book of Jonah recorded:

And the word of the LORD came unto Jonah ... Go unto Nineveh, that great city, and preach unto it the preaching that I bid thee. So Jonah arose, and went unto Nineveh, according to the word of the LORD ... and he cried ... Yet forty days, and Nineveh shall be overthrown ...

So the people of Nineveh believed God, and proclaimed a fast, and put on sackcloth, from the greatest of them even to the least of

> them ... And God saw their works,
> that they turned from their evil way;
> and God repented of the evil, that he
> had said that he would do unto them;
> and he did it not. (Jonah 3)

If you reject God's will and make selfish choices, the Holy Spirit convicts you in your heart to repent and be forgiven, and instead of the consequences you deserve, you can trust in Him to redeem your mistakes. Then, He will turn the situation around and bless you — He only asks that you have faith in Him to do it:

> And we know that God causes all
> things to work together for good to those
> who love God, to those who are called
> according to His purpose. (Romans 8:28)

If you have done bad things, or if bad things have been done to you, the Lord can ransom you, not just from hell, but from hell on Earth. The root word of salvation is salvage. Jesus is our salvation-—and He is also our salvager. He can salvage your life from the pit of destruction and make something beautiful out of your life. He can give you "beauty for ashes" (Isaiah 61:3).

He can save you from attacks of the devil, and He can save you from predicaments you got yourself into without any help from the devil. You can have faith that the Holy Spirit goes before you to lead you, and then goes behind you to straighten out the messes you got yourself into when you didn't follow His leading.

God can erase hurtful words spoken in selfish rage and heal the brokenhearted. "A bruised reed he will not break, and a smoldering wick he will not snuff out" (Isaiah 42:3) In Luke 4:18-19, Jesus opened the scroll and read from the Prophet Isaiah:

> The Spirit of the Lord is upon me, because he hath anointed me to preach the gospel to the poor; he hath sent me to heal the brokenhearted, to preach deliverance to the captives, and recovering of sight to the blind, to set at liberty them that are bruised.

> Psalm 34:18-19 states: The Lord is nigh unto them that are of a broken heart; and saveth such as be of a contrite spirit. Many are the afflictions of the righteous: but the Lord delivereth him out of them all.

God limits the options from which we choose. Exodus 13:17: "It came to pass, when Pharaoh had let the people go, that God did not lead them by way of the land of the Philistines, although that was near; for God said, 'Lest perhaps the people change their minds when they see war, and return to Egypt.'"

If you have a GPS app on your iPhone and you make a wrong turn, it will instantly recalculate and get you to your destination by a different route. What if lots of people are using the app and make wrong turns? It can recalculate everyone's routes simultaneously. What if every human on Earth is making wrong turns?

If you miss the leading of the Holy Spirit and make wrong turns and sin, you repent, trust God, and He will get you to the destination He has for your life, even though it may be through a different route. "In all your ways acknowledge Him and He will direct your path." (Proverbs 3:6) God exists outside of time and, as mentioned earlier He can adjust every single atom in the universe so that His ultimate will takes place.

> I am God, and there is no other ... declaring the end from the beginning, and from ancient times the things that are not yet done, saying ... I will do all my pleasure ... I have spoken it, I will also bring it to pass; I have purposed it, I will also do it. (Isaiah 46:9-11)

> The Lord of hosts hath sworn, saying, Surely as I have thought, so shall it come to pass; and as I have purposed, so shall it stand ... This is the purpose that is purposed upon the whole earth ... For the Lord of hosts hath purposed, and who shall disannul it? (Isaiah 14:24-27)

> Then Job replied to the Lord: I know that you can do all things; no purpose of yours can be thwarted.

(Job 42:1-2)

I the LORD have spoken it: it shall come to pass, and I will do it. (Ezekiel 24:14)

There is no wisdom, no understanding, and no plan against the LORD. (Proverbs 21:30)

Heaven and earth will pass away, but my words will not pass away. (Matthew 24:35)

He can even use the wrath of man to praise Him (Psalm 76:10). God knows what evil acts people will do and uses them for His purposes. Joseph's brothers sold him into slavery in Egypt, but he told them:

As for you, you meant evil against me, but God meant it for good, to bring it about that many people should be kept alive, as they are today. (Genesis 50:20)

God's redemption always makes things better than they were before. Mankind fell when Adam and Eve sinned, but God did not just restore us to being naked in the Garden, He made things better — He adopted us as sons and daughters, made us children of God, joint heirs with Christ, filled us with the Holy Spirit, and given us intimate fellowship with Him.

♦

WORSHIP IS RETURNING YOUR LIFE TO GOD

When we worship God, we are giving back to Him the life He gave to us.

> Ecclesiastes 1:6-7 states: "The wind goeth toward the south, and turneth about unto the north ... the wind returneth again according to his circuits. All the rivers run into the sea; yet the sea is not full; unto the place from whence the rivers come, thither they return again."

> Isaiah 55:10-11 states: "For as the rain cometh down, and the snow from heaven, and returneth not thither, but watereth the earth, and maketh it bring forth and bud, that it may give seed to the sower, and bread to the eater: So shall my word be that goeth forth out of my mouth: it shall not return unto me void, but it shall accomplish that which I please, and it shall prosper in the thing whereto I sent it."

God lends His existence to create things. There is no other place for "existence" to come from other than from God Himself. He revealed His name to Moses "I AM THAT I AM." Bible commentators explain this also carries the meaning, "He who causes everything to be."

George MacDonald wrote:

> If we do not die to ourselves,
> we cannot live to God, and he that
> does not live to God, is dead.

Life comes from God and must return to God. There is no life in the universe other than God's, so for anything to be exist and be alive, that life must come from Him and eventually return to Him. Our life returns to Him, not in the pagan animist sense of the circle of life, or in the Hindu nirvana sense of ceasing to exist as an individual and be absorbed into Vishnu, but in the biblical sense—where you retain your individuality and meet your Maker:

> Prepare to meet thy God (Amos 4:12)

> So then every one of us shall give account of himself to God. (Romans 4:12)

> My desire is to depart and be with Christ, for that is far better. (Philippians 1:23)

Life exists in the flow through. A tree is alive as water comes up from the roots and evaporates through the leaves. The Earth has a North Pole and a South Pole, with a magnetic field which flows in a circle from one pole to the other, as can be detected with a compass. Similarly, a battery has a negative terminal and a positive terminal, with an electric charge going from one end to the other.

A lamp has a cord which plugs into an outlet. At the end of cord there are two prongs. What if only one prong went into the outlet, would the lamp or appliance turn on? No. Both prongs need to plug in to complete the circuit. If we apply this analogy to our spiritual relationship with God—the "charge" of His love is sent out to our hearts, and when we accept it and return the love and glory back to Him, it completes the circuit, and our spiritual light bulb turns on — we become spiritually alive, born again. Think of prayer as recharging your spiritual battery, plugging into God, the eternal source of life.

You will find true happiness, joy and purpose in life when you let God's love into your heart and then let it flow back to Him in worship and by loving others.

Saint Augustine wrote in his *Confessions* (397-400 A.D.):

> You have made us for yourself,
> O Lord, and our heart is restless
> until it rests in you.

C.S. Lewis wrote in *Mere Christianity,* 1942:

> God made us: invented us as
> a man invents an engine. A car is
> made to run on petrol, and it would
> not run properly on anything else.
> Now God designed the human
> machine to run on Himself. He
> Himself is the fuel our spirits were
> designed to burn, or the food our
> spirits were designed to feed on.
> There is no other.

That is why it is just no good asking God to make us happy in our own way without bothering about religion. God cannot give us a happiness and peace apart from Himself, because it is not there. There is no such thing.

Ecclesiastes 3:11 (Amplified Bible) states:

He has made everything beautiful and appropriate in its time. He has also planted eternity [a sense of divine purpose] in the human heart [a mysterious longing which nothing under the sun can satisfy, except God].

If we stiffen our necks, harden our hearts, repel God's love and refuse to give glory back to Him in worship, then the circuit is not completed – we have no spiritual life. The Dead Sea has water go into it, but the water does not come out, so it is dead – the salt content is so high nothing can live in or around it. When someone is selfish, and takes in but does not give out, that person is spiritually dead.

The Book of Daniel, chapters 4-5, tell of Nebuchadnezzar walking on his palace walls, saying, "Is not this great Babylon, that I have built ... by the might of my power, and for the honor of my majesty?" But when he did not give glory back to God "there fell a voice from heaven, saying, O king Nebuchadnezzar ... The kingdom is departed from thee. And they shall drive thee from men, and thy dwelling shall be with the beasts of the field." "When his heart was lifted up, and his mind hardened in pride, he was deposed from his kingly throne."

Later, Daniel told Nebuchadnezzar's son: "And thou his son, O Belshazzar, hast not humbled thine heart, though thou knewest all this; but hast lifted up thyself against the Lord of heaven; and they have brought the vessels of his house before thee, and thou, and thy lords, thy wives, and thy concubines, have drunk wine in them ... and the God in whose hand thy breath is ... thou not glorified: Then was the part of the hand sent from him; and this writing was written ... God hath numbered thy kingdom, and finished it."

Herod gave a speech to the people of Tyre and Sidon, who replied "'the voice of a god, and not of a man' ... Immediately the angel of the Lord smote Herod, because he gave not God the glory ... and gave up the ghost." (Acts 12)

Lucifer was the most beautiful angel who experienced life from God, but his heart was "lifted up," he refused to give the glory back to God, and pridefully boasted "I will exalt my throne above the stars of God ... I will be like the most High."

As a result, he was cast out "Yet thou shalt be brought down to hell, to the sides of the pit." Lucifer spiritually short-circuited and was shot out of heaven like a blown fuse, like lightning. (Isaiah 14:9-17; Ezekiel 28:5-10; Luke 10:19)

Worship is giving honor, respect, reverence, devotion, profound admiration, and homage. God gave us life—our worship is us giving our lives back to Him.

The more life and blessings God gives you, the more you are to give the glory back to Him in worship — and the brighter your light will shine! Moses spent so much time with God that his face shone with light. Exodus 34:29 described: "Moses did not know that the skin of his face shone because of His speaking with Him."

We join all creation in giving glory back to God in worship, but we as humans can do something more – we can love Him back for redeeming us!

Wouldn't you rather believe that there is an All-Powerful, Perfectly Just God who created you in His image, who loved you enough to send His only begotten Son to die for your sins, who desires you to love Him back, who fills you with the Holy Spirit so He can love others through you, and who has planned for you an eternity of joy with Him.

Wouldn't rather believe that than coldly imagine all the complexities of the universe were the result of a brainless random chance; that your life is a purposeless accident; that what is good and beauty in life is a fluke; that there is no right or wrong; that survival of the fittest permits the strong to crush the weak; and that there is nothing to look forward to but empty nothingness.

French mathematician Blaise Pascal (1623-1662) was known for "Pascal's Wager":

> How can anyone lose who chooses to become a Christian? If, when he dies, there turns out to be no God and his faith was in vain, he has lost nothing — in fact, he has been happier in life than his non-believing friends.
>
> If, however, there is a God and a heaven and hell, then he has gained heaven and his skeptical friends will have lost everything in hell!

At the end of Frank Capra's classic 1946 movie, *It's a Wonderful Life*, the distraught George Bailey thought the world would be better off if he had never existed, but an angel showed him how God used him to change people's lives for the better, then he cried out:

> Please! Please! I wanna live again. I wanna live again. Please, God, let me live again!

♦

THROUGH OUR TRIALS WE LOOK FORWARD TO HEAVEN

C.S. Lewis wrote:

> If I find in myself desires which nothing in this world can

satisfy, the only logical explanation
is that I was made for another world.

After the trials of our lives on Earth,
we will have eternal joy with Jesus and Our
Father in heaven.

> Blessed are you when men hate
> you, And when they exclude you, And
> revile you, and cast out your name
> as evil, For the Son of Man's sake.
> Rejoice in that day and leap for joy!
> For indeed your reward is great in
> heaven. (Luke 6:22-23)

> For our light affliction, which is
> but for a moment, is working for us a
> far more exceeding and eternal weight
> of glory, while we do not look at the
> things which are seen, but at the things
> which are not seen. For the things
> which are seen are temporary, but the
> things which are not seen are eternal.
> (2 Corinthians 4:17)

> Beloved, think it not strange
> concerning the fiery trial which is
> to try you, as though some strange
> thing happened unto you: But rejoice,
> inasmuch as ye are partakers of
> Christ's sufferings; that, when his
> glory shall be revealed, ye may be glad
> also with exceeding joy. (I Peter 4:12)

> These things I have spoken unto

you, that in me ye might have peace. In the world ye shall have tribulation: but be of good cheer; I have overcome the world. (John 16:33)

Let not your heart be troubled; you believe in God, believe also in Me. In My Father's house are many mansions; if it were not so, I would have told you. I go to prepare a place for you. And if I go and prepare a place for you, I will come again and receive you to Myself; that where I am, there you may be also. (John 14:1-3)

Eye hath not seen, nor ear heard, neither have entered into the heart of man, the things which God hath prepared for them that love him. (1 Corinthians 2:9; Isaiah 64:4)

For He Himself has said, "I will never leave you nor forsake you." (Hebrews 13:5)

And, lo, I am with you always. (Matthew 28:20)

♦

WORTHY IS THE LAMB
In heaven we will join with saints and angels in worshiping God. The Book of Revelation describes:

Then I looked, and I heard the

voice of many angels around the throne, the living creatures, and the elders; and the number of them was ten thousand times ten thousand, and thousands of thousands, saying with a loud voice: "Worthy is the Lamb who was slain, to receive power and riches and wisdom, And strength and honor and glory and blessing!"

And every creature which is in heaven and on the earth and under the earth and such as are in the sea, and all that are in them, I heard saying: "Blessing and honor and glory and power Be to Him who sits on the throne, And to the Lamb, forever and ever!" ...

And I John saw the holy city, new Jerusalem, coming down from God out of heaven, prepared as a bride adorned for her husband. And I heard a great voice out of heaven saying,

"Behold, the tabernacle of God is with men, and he will dwell with them, and they shall be his people, and God himself shall be with them, and be their God. And God shall wipe away all tears from their eyes; and there shall be no more death, neither sorrow, nor crying, neither shall there be any more pain: for the former things are passed away."

And he that sat upon the throne
said, "Behold, I make all things new."

∽

WHAT IS YOUR STORY?

Someday you will be dead — but you will be in heaven because you believe that Jesus died on the cross to pay for all of your sins.

And as the song *Amazing Grace* goes, "When we've been there ten thousand years, bright shining as the sun, we've no less days to sing God's praise, than when we've first begun!"

Imagine being in heaven ten thousand years, walking on the streets of gold, and you get a chance to meet Moses. That would be pretty amazing! Maybe Moses will invite you over to his place. I don't know what it is like in heaven, but I bet Moses will have a pretty nice place. Jesus did say, "In my Father's house are many mansions." (John 14:2)

Moses will probably a big living room with one of those fireplaces where the logs don't burn up — (remember, he saw the burning bush in the wilderness that didn't burn up!) Imagine lots of people show up there.

I heard someone say, in heaven you will probably be able to travel as fast as you think — and I will probably show up late. My wife will say, where were you? And I will answer – umm, I was thinking of something else.

Anyway, imagine we are all there, and after

all the small talk, you just can't contain yourself. You say — Moses, tell us the story, what was it like? I read the book, I even saw the movie, but here you are in person.

Moses will stand up, the room will get quiet, and he will say, I was 80 years old, and Pharaoh, with the most powerful army in the world at the time, was charging in on us. We were totally unarmed. It looked hopeless! But I held out my staff and said, God use me to deliver your people! Then the waves came in and swallowed up Pharaoh's chariots!

Everyone in the room will be in awe!

Then you look around the room and see David, and say — David, tell us your story. He will stand up, the room will get quiet, and he will say, I was just a teenager, and this giant thug Goliath was mocking our God, mocking our faith, and the grownups were too chicken to do anything. So I said, enough of this. I took my sling and hit him in the head with a stone, then took his own sword and chopped his head off.

And everyone in the room will be in awe!

Then you look around and see Gideon, and say, — Gideon, tell us your story. He will stand up and tell his story — There were 120,000 Midianites and I had 32,000 Israelites, and God said — Too many. Tell everyone that's scared to go home. Great — now I only had 10,000 Israelites. God said — still too many. Have them drink from a creek. And he whittled the number down to 300. Then God rolled up his sleeves and said – Watch this! And with just 300, we defeated the Midianite host.

Everyone in the room will be in awe!

One by one, everyone in Moses living room will tell their story. It will be exciting to hear Joshua, Rahab, Deborah, Elijah, Elisha, John the Baptist, the Apostle Paul ...

Then everyone in the room will stop and look directly at YOU and say—You, we haven't heard from you yet! Tell us your story!

What are you going to say?

Will it be something lame, like, well, I threw a couple bucks in the offering plate, or I turned the channel when something bad came on.

I would hate for Jesus to walk in room, and there be a big screen come down showing all kinds of tremendous miracles and crowds coming to the Lord, and Him turning to you and saying — This is what I had planned for you to do when you were on Earth, but you just didn't have enough faith and courage.

And you look back at your life, and see that big mountain that held you back, and you're shocked to see it was just a tiny anthill. And you say to yourself, — Oh no, I let that tiny anthill, that fear of man, that worry about what people are going to think about me, hold me back from doing all those great things for the Lord!

And you can't go back to Earth to do anything else for the Lord, because you are already in heaven, because you believe that Jesus died on the cross to pay for all your sins!

But guess what, you are still on this Earth, you still have breath in your lungs, you still have feet that trod the soil, you still can do all those things that you will be known for forever!

Moses will always be known for standing up to Pharaoh; David will always be known for standing up to Goliath; and you will always be known for what you are doing for the Lord right now!

This is an exciting time to be alive!

Out of the 6,000 years of recorded human history, God decided for you to be alive at this specific time! He knows all the corruption in the world, all the dirty backroom deals by corrupt politicians, and all the evil globalist plots to rule the world, and He thinks you have got what it takes to overcome them!

He has given you His Word, He has given you the Holy Spirit, He has given you great pastors, gifted teachers and Christian friends!

It is like Jesus is the Basketball Coach, and you are a player sitting on the bench, and He comes over and slaps you on the back and says, — It is your turn, get in the game.

And you respond — but Coach, they are playing really tough out there! And He says, — Yes, I know. Now it is your turn. Get in the game. And you say, — but Coach, someone just got knocked down!

And He says, — yes, I know ... but they are four feet tall and you are six feet tall! You can do this!!! Now, get in the game!

"Greater is he that is in you, than he that is in the world." (1John.4:4)

"Fear not ... I am thy shield, and thy exceeding great reward." (Genesis 15:1)

"Fear not, nor be dismayed, be strong and of good courage." (Joshua 10:25)

"Fear not: for I have redeemed thee, I have called thee by thy name; thou art mine." (Isaiah 43:1)

"No weapon that is formed against thee shall prosper; and every tongue that shall rise against thee in judgment thou shalt condemn. This is the heritage of the servants of the LORD, and their righteousness is of me, saith the LORD." (Isaiah 54:17)

"Thou shalt not be afraid ... A thousand shall fall at thy side, and ten thousand at thy right hand; but it shall not come nigh thee." (Psalm 91:5-7)

"When the enemy shall come in like a flood, the Spirit of the LORD shall lift up a standard against him." (Isaiah 59:19)

"The righteous are bold as a lion." (Prov. 28:1)

"Every place that the sole of your foot shall tread upon, that have I given unto you ... There shall not any man be able to stand before thee ... I will be with thee: I will not fail thee, nor forsake thee. Be strong and of a good courage." (Joshua 1:3-7)

The Lord chose for you to be alive on the Earth at this exact time. He knows every situation you are facing. He loves you and will protect you. If you seek Him, seek Him, seek Him, with all your heart, and He gives you even just a tiny glimpse of the endless love He has for you, your life will be changed forever!

> You will seek Me and find Me,
> when you search for Me with all
> your heart. (Jeremiah 29:13)

God has a plan for your life! Trust Him. This is your time to shine, to do those things for the Lord that you will be known for eternity! "Be thou strong and very courageous!" God is with you!

SELECTED SCRIPTURES & QUOTATIONS

&

BELIEVE GOD HAS A PLAN FOR YOUR LIFE

Scriptures to believe in:

> In everything you do, put God
> first and He will direct you and
> crown your efforts with success.
> (Proverbs 3:6 NIV)

The plan for your life should always be based on what you believe is God's will for you. He has given you specific gifts and talents, likes and dislikes that will help you to determine what you could do successfully and happily.

♦

> A man without self-control is
> as defenseless as a city with broken-
> down walls. (Proverbs 25:28 TLB)

You must discipline yourself to work to achieve your goals every day. Every moment is a precious gift from God and once spent can never be retrieved. So make the most of every moment and every talent that God has given you.

♦

"Prayer is not trying to twist God's arm to

make Him do something. Prayer is receiving by faith what He has already done."—Andrew Wommack

♦

> If you want favor with both God and man, and a reputation for good judgment and common sense, then trust the Lord completely. (Proverbs 3:4-5 TLB)

Make sure that you begin each day with a prayer asking the Lord to guide you and dedicating each day to His service. He will bring the people and ideas that you need if you listen to God.

Applying this to business or school, written records are always a good idea when making important decisions. They will be references to see how God has led you and remind you of why you made those decisions at the time. They will help you to make wiser decisions in the future.

♦

"Everyday without exception—is a gift from God, entrusted to us to use for His Glory."—Billy Graham

♦

> Lies will get any man into trouble but honesty is its own defense. (Proverbs 12:13 TLB)

♦

> Any story sounds true until

someone tells the other side and
sets the record straight. (Proverbs
18:17 TLB)

One must always remain honest to
himself and to God. Do not be tempted to lie
or deceive. One lie leads to another and then
you can be trapped by your own lies. Once
trust is broken, it is very hard to be restored.
There is always a freedom in telling the truth.
Virtue is its own reward.

♦

A lazy fellow has trouble all
through life; the good man's path is
easy. (Proverbs 15:19 TLB)

You must always take responsibility for
making the commitment to put the necessary
time and energy into your projects. You must
plan and organize. Make sure that you follow
through on each step and the outcome will be
what you wanted to achieve.

♦

Putting confidence in an
unreliable man is like chewing
with a sore tooth or trying to run
on a broken foot. (Proverbs 25:19)

You want to always be reliable. If you say
that you will do something, do it to the best
of your ability. Have you ever felt the hurt of
broken promises? People remember those that
cause them pain and will not trust them again.

♦

Be patient and you will finally
win, for a soft tongue can break hard
bones. (Proverbs 25:15)

Do not get anxious and say things that you will regret. Think first and always respond with kind words and they will make a way for you. Always thank others for kindnesses shared and they will be multiplied back to you.

◆

A faithful employee is as
refreshing as a cool day in the hot
summertime. (Proverbs 25:13)

It is such a delight to be able to count on someone to do the job to their utmost abilities and not have to worry if the task will be completed. Always do your job well, whether you feel like it or not. Satisfaction and fulfillment will be your great reward.

◆

A wise man is mightier that a
strong man. Wisdom is mightier than
strength. (Proverbs 24:5)

Learn all that you can to be the best at what you do. That wisdom will guide you to the top and can never be taken away from you. Use action-oriented words to help demonstrate what you have actually accomplished and what you are capable of. Keep numbers substantiating your successes!

◆

It is an honor for a man to stay out of a fight. Only fools insist on quarreling. (Proverbs 20:3)

♦

A wise man restrains his anger and overlooks insults. This is to his credit. (Proverbs 19:11)

♦

"What really matters is what happens in us, not to us."— D. James Kennedy

♦

It is always better to rise above an argument. Never use words to instigate anger in others. Let your words be filled with kindness and encouragement. If someone tries to fight with you, do as Jesus said and turn the other cheek. Their anger will be dispelled, and they will be ashamed. You will be the noble one who took the high road.

♦

If you will not plow in the cold, you will not eat at harvest. (Proverbs 20:4)

You must plan ahead and be prepared for the future seasons of life. You must keep working toward living a fruitful life. Hard work is always rewarded in due season. At work, you should make contributions to both profit and efficiency. Make sure that something is accomplished just because you are there. Use the same resources to achieve more. You have more skills than you realize. As you review your accomplishments, your abilities and talents will surface.

♦

> The Lord despises every kind of cheating. (Proverbs 20:10)

♦

> It is wrong to accept a bribe and twist justice. Others may not know that you cheated but the Lord sees everything you do (Proverbs 17:23).

♦

> For the eyes of the Lord run to and fro throughout the whole earth, to show Himself strong on behalf of them whose heart is perfect toward Him. (2 Chronicles 16:9)

♦

> Good sense is far more valuable than gold or precious jewels. (Proverbs 20:15 TLB)

Gold and jewels may be pretty but can be stolen. No one can take good sense from you and it can be shared throughout your lifetime.

♦

> There are friends who pretend to be friends, but there is a Friend who sticks closer than a brother. (Proverbs 18:24)

You can always trust God and give your thoughts to him in prayer. If you have a hesitation in your heart about sharing something with a friend, it is probably the Holy Spirit gentling leading you not to. Remember that no matter what happens, the Lord is your friend in time of need. Always take your concerns to Him Who cares for you.

♦

The wise man is glad to be instructed, but a self-sufficient fool falls flat on his face (Proverbs 10:8).

♦

Anyone willing to be corrected is on the pathway to life. Anyone refusing has lost his chance. (Proverbs 10:17)

Sometimes our generation does not appreciate the wisdom gained through life experiences of the generations before us. If a senior at work or home offers advice to help us, we should appreciate it and seriously consider what they are saying. Those who have the courage to correct us are those who really care to help improve our life or situation. Correction is a good thing—at work, home or school. Use it to become all that you can be.

♦

A wise man holds his tongue.
Only a fool blurts out everything

he knows: that only leads to sorrow
and trouble. (Proverbs 10:14)

Sometimes, we can say too much.
Always consider your words carefully before
you offer advice. Some thoughts are meant to
be for our hearts only. Pray that God gives you
daily wisdom to say only what you should.
Never say anything unkind about anyone. Be
a person of few words, but of great wisdom.

♦

Jesus said, all things are possible
to those who believe. (Mark 9:23)

♦

All things are possible with
God. (Mark 10:27)

♦

Whatsoever you ask for in
prayer, believe that you have received
it and it is yours. (Mark 11:24)

♦

For it is God who works in you
to will and to act according to His
good purpose. (Philippians 2:13)

❧

QUOTATIONS ON WHAT INSPIRED THE SUCCESSFUL

On August 3, 1492, Columbus set sail and after the longest voyage ever made out of sight of land, discovered the New World on October 12, 1492. In his *Libro de las profecias* (*Book of Prophecies*), written between his third and fourth voyages, Christopher Columbus wrote:

> Our Lord wished to perform the clearest miracle in this of the voyage to the Indies, to console me and others:

> I spent seven years in your royal Court arguing the case with so many persons of such authority and learned in all the arts, and in the end they concluded that all was idle nonsense, and with this they gave up; yet the outcome will be the fulfillment of what our Redeemer Jesus Christ said, and had said beforehand by the mouth of his Holy Prophets.

And so there is every reason to believe that this other will become manifest; and being sure of what we hope for, if what said done not suffice, I offer as support the holy Gospel, in which Jesus stated that everything would pass away, but not his wonderful Word; and with this he said that it was utterly necessary for all that was written by him and by the prophets to be fulfilled.

◆

Sir Isaac Newton was a renowned mathematician who formulated the laws of motion, law of universal gravitation, laws of optics, and was a discoverer of calculus. He wrote:

There is one God, the Father, ever-living, omnipresent, omniscient, almighty, the Maker of heaven and earth, and one Mediator between God and man, the man Christ Jesus .... To us there is but one God, the Father, of whom are all things.

◆

William Penn, who founded Pennsylvania, wrote in his *Treatise on the Religion of the Quakers*:

I do declare to the whole world that we believe the Scriptures to contain a declaration of the mind and will of God in and to those ages in which they were written; being given forth by the Holy Ghost moving in the hearts of holy men of God; that they ought also to be read, believed, and fulfilled in our day; being used for reproof and instruction, that the man of God may be perfect.

They are a declaration and testimony of heavenly things themselves, and, as such, we carry a high respect for them. We accept them as the words of God Himself.

♦

Rev. Samuel Provoost, the first U.S. Senate Chaplain, stated on Sunday, July 15, 1787, in the first ordination sermon in St. George's Chapel, New York City:

Let no Man despise thy youth, but be thou an Example of the Believers in Word, in Conversation, in Charity, in Spirit, in Faith, in Purity. Give Attendance to reading and to exhortation. Take Heed unto thyself and unto thy Doctrine; for in doing this, thou shall both save thyself and them that hear thee.

♦

President Thomas Jefferson stated in his 8th Annual Message, November 8, 1808:

> Earnestly praying, as we are in duty bound, that the Supreme Lawgiver of the Universe by illuminating those to whom it is addressed, may, on the one hand, turn their councils from every act which would affront His holy prerogative, or violate the trust committed to them; and, on the other, guide them into every measure which may be worthy of His blessing.

♦

Benjamin Franklin stated at the Constitutional Convention, April 17, 1787:

> We have been assured, Sir, in the sacred writings, that "except the Lord build the House they labor in vain that build it. I firmly believe this," and I also believe that without his concurring aid we shall succeed in this political building no better, than the Builders of Babel:
>
> We shall be divided by our little partial local interests; our projects will be confounded, and we ourselves shall become a reproach and bye word down to future ages.

And what is worse, mankind may hereafter from this unfortunate instance, despair of establishing Governments by Human wisdom and leave it to chance, war and conquest.

I therefore beg leave to move— that henceforth prayers imploring the assistance of Heaven, and its blessings on our deliberations, be held in this Assembly every morning before we proceed to business, and that one or more of the Clergy of this City be requested to officiate in that Service.

♦

Missionary to India William Carey established the first modern Protestant Christian mission in the non-English-speaking world—the Serampore Mission near Calcutta. He declared in a sermon, May 30, 1792:

Expect great things from God.
Attempt great things for God.

♦

Richard Johnson was the first chaplain to the Colony of New South Wales, Australia, recommended to that position by anti-slavery champions William Wilberforce and John Newton. Rev. Richard Johnson stated in 1792:

The gospel ... proposes a free and gracious pardon to the guilty, cleansing to the polluted, healing to the sick, happiness to the miserable, light for those who sit in darkness, strength for the weak, food for the hungry, and even life for the dead.

♦

William Samuel Johnson was a Signer of the U.S. Constitution. As president of Columbia University (formerly King's College), he addressed the first graduating class after the Revolutionary War:

You this day, gentlemen, assume new characters, enter into new relations, and consequently incur new duties. You have, by the favor of Providence and the attention of friends, received a public education, the purpose whereof hath been to qualify you the better to serve your Creator and your country ...

Your first great duties, you are sensible, are those you owe to Heaven, to your Creator and Redeemer. Let these be ever present to your minds and exemplified in your lives and conduct. Imprint deep upon your minds the principles of piety towards God, and a reverence and fear of His holy name.

The fear of God is the beginning of wisdom and its consummation is everlasting felicity. Possess yourselves of just and elevated notions of the Divine character, attributes, and administration, and of the end and dignity of your own immortal nature as it stands related to Him.

Reflect deeply and often upon those relations. Remember that it is in God you live and move and have your being,—that in the language of David He is about your bed and about your path and spieth out all your ways,—that there is not a thought in your hearts, nor a word upon your tongues, but lo! He knoweth them altogether, and that he will one day call you to a strict account for all your conduct in this mortal life.

Remember, too, that you are the redeemed of the Lord, that you are bought with a price, even the inestimable price of the precious blood of the Son of God.

Adore Jehovah, therefore, as your God and your Judge. Love,

fear, and serve Him as your Creator, Redeemer, and Sanctifier. Acquaint yourselves with Him in His word and holy ordinances.

Make Him your friend and protector and your felicity is secured both here and hereafter. And with respect to particular duties to Him, it is your happiness that you are well assured that he best serves his Maker, who does most good to his country and to mankind.

♦

President James Madison issued a Proclamation of a National Day of Thanksgiving, March 4, 1815:

The Senate and House of Representatives of the United States ... recommended to be observed by the people of the United States with religious solemnity as a day of thanksgiving and of devout acknowledgments to Almighty God for His great goodness manifested in restoring to them the blessing of peace.

No people ought to feel greater obligations to celebrate the goodness of the Great Disposer of Events and of the Destiny of Nations than the people of the United States.

His kind providence originally conducted them to one of the best portions of the dwelling place allotted for the great family of the human race. He protected and cherished them under all the difficulties and trials to which they were exposed in their early days.

Under His fostering care their habits, their sentiments, and their pursuits prepared them for a transition in due time to a state of independence and self-government. In the arduous struggle by which it was attained they were distinguished by multiplied tokens of His benign interposition.

♦

English scientist Michael Faraday, renowned for his discoveries in electromagnetism, stated:

The Bible, and it alone, with nothing added to it nor taken away from it by man, is the sole and sufficient guide for each individual, at all times and in all circumstances ... Faith in the divinity and work of Christ is the gift of God, and evidence of this faith is obedience to the commandment of Christ.

♦

John Greenleaf Whittier is one of the first to suggest that an anti-slavery party should be created – the Republican Party. He wrote:

> I believe in the Scriptures because they repeat the warnings and promises of the indwelling Light and Truth; I find in them the eternal precepts of the Divine Spirit declared and repeated. They testify of Christ within ...
>
> My ground of hope for myself and for humanity is in that Divine fullness which was manifested in the life, teachings, and self-sacrifice of Christ. In the infinite mercy of God so revealed, and not in any work or merit of my own nature, I humbly, yet very hopefully, trust.

◆

President Abraham Lincoln, who championed ending slavery in America by issuing the Emancipation Proclamation and working to pass the 13th Amendment, stated in 1864:

> I believe in national humiliation, fasting, and prayer, in keeping a day holy to the Lord, devoted to the humble discharge of the religious duties proper to such a solemn occasion ...

I believe in Him whose will, not ours, should be done. I believe the people of the United States, in the forms approved by their own consciences, should render the homage due to the Divine Majesty for the wonderful things He has done in the nation's behalf, and invoke the influence of His Holy Spirit to subdue anger ...

I believe in His eternal truth and justice. I believe the will of God prevails; without Him all human reliance is vain; without the assistance of that Divine Being I cannot succeed; with that assistance I cannot fail.

I believe I am a humble instrument in the hands of our Heavenly Father; I desire that all my works and acts may be according to His will; and that it may be so, I give thanks to the Almighty and seek His aid. I believe in praise to Almighty God, the beneficent Creator and Ruler of the Universe.

♦

President Abraham Lincoln stated in his Second Inaugural Address, March 4, 1865, just 45 days before his assassination:

God has given me what He has

in trust to make of it a contribution to the world far greater than money can for myself. Yes, my friend, I think I understood you.

My letter to you probably was not as clear as it should have been. I believe that science (truth) if it will take what you have had revealed to you. Search and continue to search. I am sure they will find a world of truth in it.

♦

Theodore Roosevelt wrote in *The Works of Theodore Roosevelt*, Vol. IX-The Winning of the West—An account of the exploration and settlement of our country from the Alleghenies to the Pacific (NY: Charles Scribner's Sons, 1926, p. 43):

All the religion I have is to love and fear God, believe in Jesus Christ, do all the good to my neighbors and myself that I can, and do as little harm as I can help, and trust on God's mercy for the rest.

♦

George Washington Carver, while a student at Simpson College, ended his letter to John and Helen Milholland, 1890:

My best respects to all. I remain your humble servant of God.

I am learning to trust and realize the blessed results from trusting in Him every day. I am glad to hear of your advancement spiritually and financially. I regard them also as especial blessings from God.

Dr. Carver exclaimed humorously, speaking in the summer of 1920:

"I always look forward to introductions as opportunities to learn something about myself."

He continued: "Years ago I went into my laboratory and said, 'Dear Mr. Creator, please tell me what the universe was made for?'

The Great Creator answered, 'You want to know too much for that little mind of yours. Ask for something more your size, little man.

Then I asked. 'Please, Mr. Creator, tell me what man was made for.'

Again the Great Creator replied, 'You are still asking too much. Cut down on the extent and improve the intent.'

So then I asked, 'Please, Mr. Creator, will you tell me why the peanut was made?'

'That's better, but even then it's infinite. What do you want to know about the peanut?'

'Mr. Creator, can I make milk out of the peanut?'

'What kind of milk do you want? Good Jersey milk or just plain boarding house milk?'

'Good Jersey milk.'

And then the Great Creator taught me to take the peanut apart and put it together again. And out of the process have come forth all these products!"

♦

President Woodrow Wilson stated September 8, 1914:

Therefore, I, Woodrow Wilson, President of the United States of America, do designate ... a day of prayer and supplication and do request all God-fearing persons to repair on that day to their places of worship there to unite their petitions to Almighty God that, overruling the counsel of men, setting straight the things they cannot govern or alter, taking pity on the nations now in the throes of conflict, in His mercy and goodness showing a way where men can see none,

He vouchsafe His children healing peace again and restore once more that concord among men and nations without which there can be neither happiness nor true friendship nor any wholesome fruit of toil or thought in the world;

Praying also to this end that He forgive us our sins, our ignorance of His holy will, our willfulness and many errors, a of His holy will, our willfulness and many errors, and lead us in the paths of obedience to places of vision and to thoughts and counsels that purge and make wise.

We mourn with those who have suffered great and disastrous loss. All our hearts have been seared by the sudden and sense-less taking of innocent lives.

We pray for healing and for the strength to serve and encourage one another in hope and faith. Scripture says: "Blessed are those who mourn for they shall be comforted."

I call on every American

family and the family of America to observe a National Day of Prayer and Remembrance, honoring the memory of the thousands of victims of these brutal attacks and comforting those who lost loved ones.

We will persevere through this national tragedy and personal loss. In time, we will find healing and recovery; and, in the face of all this evil, we remain strong and united, "one Nation under God."

◆

President Franklin D. Roosevelt stated November 8, 1941:

I ... do hereby designate and set aside Thursday, the twentieth day of November, 1941, as a day to be observed in giving thanks to the Heavenly Source of our earthly blessings ... We are grateful to the Father of us all for the innumerable daily manifestations of His beneficent mercy in affairs both public and private, for the bounties of the harvest, for opportunities to labor and to serve, and for the continuance of those homely joys and satisfactions which enrich our lives.

Let us ask the Divine Blessing
on our decision and determination
to protect our way of life against
the forces of evil and slavery which
seek in these days to encompass us.

On the day appointed for
this purpose, let us reflect at our
homes or places of worship on the
goodness of God and, in giving
thanks, let us pray for a speedy end
to strife and the establishment on
earth of freedom, brotherhood, and
justice for enduring time.

In 1980, in *The Human Life Review,*
Malcolm Muggeridge first published his
article, "The Human Holocaust," stating:

Against this vision of life without
tears in fleshly paradise, stands the
Christian vision of mankind as a
family whose loving father is God.

Here, the symbol is not the
perfected body, the pruned vine, the
weeded garden, but a stricken body
nailed to a cross, signifying affliction,
not as the enemy of life, but as its
greatest enhancement and teacher.

In an army preparing for battle
the unfit are indeed discarded, but in
a Christian family the handicapped
are particularly cherished, and give

special joy to those who cherish them.

◆

President Harry S Truman laid the cornerstone of the New York Avenue Presbyterian Church, Washington, D.C., April 3, 1951, stating:

> They gave thanks to God 'because He is good, for his mercy endureth forever.' If we hold true to our faith, as they did, I am sure that we will be able to offer, on some future day, the same heartfelt prayer of thanksgiving and joy.

◆

President Dwight Eisenhower stated June 14, 1954:

> From this day forward, the millions of our school children will daily proclaim in every city and town, every village and rural schoolhouse, the dedication of our nation and our people to the Almighty.
>
> In this way we are reaffirming the transcendence of religious faith in America's heritage and future; in this way we shall constantly strengthen those spiritual weapons which forever will be our country's most powerful resource in peace and war.

◆

"Faith and prayer are the vitamins of the soul; man cannot live in health without them."— Mahalia Jackson, influential gospel singer

♦

President Ronald Reagan stated at the National Association of Evangelicals in Orlando, Florida, March 8, 1983:

The real crisis we face today is a spiritual one; at root, it is a test of moral will and faith.

Whittaker Chambers ... wrote the crisis of the Western world exists to the degree in which the West is indifferent to God, the degree to which it collaborates in communism's attempt to make man stand alone without God ...

The source of our strength in the quest for human freedom is not material, but spiritual. And because it knows no limitation, it must terrify and ultimately triumph over those who would enslave their fellow man. For in the words of Isaiah: 'He giveth power to the faint; and to them that have no might He increases strength ...

But they that wait upon the

Lord shall renew their strength; they shall mount up with wings as eagles; they shall run, and not be weary' ... Freedom prospers when religion is vibrant and the rule of law under God is acknowledged.

When our founding fathers passed the First Amendment, they sought to protect churches from government interference. They never intended to construct a wall of hostility between government and the church.

♦

President George H.W. Bush stated, February 22, 1990, at the request of Congress, Joint Resolution 164, issued a Presidential Proclamation declaring 1990 the International Year of Bible Reading:

Among the great books produced throughout the history of mankind, the Bible has been prized above all others by generations of men and women around the world— by people of every age, every race, and every walk of life.

The Bible has had a critical impact upon the development of Western civilization. Western literature, art, and music are filled with images and ideas that can be traced to its pages.

More important, our moral tradition has been shaped by the laws and teachings it contains. It was a biblical view of man—one affirming the dignity and worth of the human person, made in the image of our Creator—that inspired the principles upon which the United States is founded.

President Jackson called the Bible "the Rock on which our Republic rests" because he knew that it shaped the Founding Fathers' concept of individual liberty and their vision of a free and just society.

The Bible has not only influenced the development of our Nation's values and institutions but also enriched the daily lives of millions of men and women who have looked to it for comfort, hope, and guidance.

On the American frontier, the Bible was often the only book a family owned. For those pioneers living far from any church or school, it served both as a source of religious instruction and as the primary text from which children learned to read.

The historic speeches of Abraham Lincoln and Dr. Martin Luther King, Jr., provide compelling evidence of the role Scripture played in shaping the struggle against slavery and discrimination. Today the Bible continues to give courage and direction to those who seek truth and righteousness.

In recognizing its enduring value, we recall the words of the prophet Isaiah, who declared, 'The grass withereth, the flower fadeth; but the word of our God shall stand forever.' Containing revelations of God's intervention in human history, the Bible offers moving testimony to His love for mankind.

Treasuring the Bible as a source of knowledge and inspiration, President Abraham Lincoln called this Great Book 'the best gift God has given to man.' President Lincoln believed that the Bible not only reveals the infinite goodness of our Creator, but also reminds us of our worth as individuals and our responsibilities toward one another.

President Woodrow Wilson likewise recognized the importance

of the Bible to its readers.

"The Bible is the word of life," he once said. Describing its contents, he added:

"You will find it full of real men and women not only but also of the things you have wondered about and been troubled about all your life, as men have been always; and the more you will read it the more it will become plain to you what things are worthwhile and what are not, what things make men happy – loyalty, right dealing, speaking the truth ... and the things that are guaranteed to make men unhappy – selfishness, cowardice, greed, and everything that is low and mean.

When you have read the Bible you will know that it is the Word of God, because you will have found it the key to your own heart, your own happiness, and your own duty."

President Wilson believed that the Bible helps its readers find answers to the mysteries and sorrows that often trouble the souls of men. Cherished for centuries by men and women around the world, the Bible's value is timeless. Its significance transcends the boundaries between nations and languages because it carries a universal message to every human heart.

This year numerous individuals and associations around the world will join in a campaign to encourage voluntary study of the Bible. Their efforts are worthy of recognition and support ... Now, Therefore, I, George Bush, President of the United States of America, do hereby proclaim the year 1990 as the "International Year of Bible Reading." I invite all Americans to discover the great inspiration and knowledge that can be obtained through thoughtful reading of the Bible.

♦

Internationally renowned neurosurgeon, Dr. Ben Caron, who served as U.S. Secretary of Housing and Urban Development, stated:

I believe if you keep your faith, you keep your trust, you keep the right attitude, if you're grateful, you'll see through hard work, perseverance, and a faith in God, you can live your dreams.

✺

BELIEVE FOR HAPPINESS, JOY & CONTENTMENT

Scriptures to believe in:

Happy is the people whose God is the Lord. (Psalm 144:15)

◆

Happy is he that hath the God of Jacob for his help, whose hope is in the Lord his God. (Psalm 146:5)

◆

Happy is the man that findeth wisdom and the man that getteth understanding ... She is more precious than rubies: and all the things thou canst desire are not to be compared to her. Length of days is in her right hand; and in her left hand, riches and honor. Her ways are the ways of pleasantness, and all her paths are peace. She is a tree of life to them that lay hold upon her: and happy is everyone that retaineth her. (Proverbs 3:13-18)

◆

He that hath mercy on the

poor, happy is he. (Proverbs 14:21)

♦

Whoso trusteth in the Lord, happy is he. (Proverbs 16:20)

♦

He that keepeth the law of God, happy is he. (Proverbs 29:8)

♦

If ye suffer for righteousness sake, happy are ye: and be not afraid of their terror, neither be troubled. (1 Peter 3:14)

♦

Blessed is everyone that feareth the Lord; that walketh in His ways. For thou shalt eat the labor of thine hands: happy shalt thou be, and it shall be well with thee. (Psalm 128:1-2)

♦

Glory and honor are in His presence and gladness are in His place. (1 Chronicles 16:27)

♦

Happy is he that hath the God of Jacob for his help, whose hope is in the LORD his God: Which made heaven, and earth, the sea, and all that therein is: which keepeth truth forever: Which executeth judgment for the oppressed: which giveth food to the hungry. The LORD looseth the prisoners: The LORD openeth the eyes of the blind: the LORD raiseth them that are bowed down: the LORD loveth the righteous: (Psalm 146:5-8)

SCRIPTURES ON JOY

He shall pray unto God, and He will be favorable unto him: and he shall see his face with joy: for He will render unto man his righteousness. (Job 33:26)

♦

Let all those that put their trust in Thee rejoice: let them ever shout for joy, because Thou defendest them; let them also that love Thy name be joyful in Thee. (Psalm 5:11)

♦

I will be glad and rejoice in Thee: I will sing praise to Thy Name, O Thou Most High. (Psalm 9:2)

♦

My heart shall rejoice in Thy salvation. (Psalm 13:15)

♦

Therefore my heart is glad and my glory rejoiceth; my flesh shall also rest in hope. Thou wilt show me the path of life: in Thy presence is fullness of joy; at Thy right hand there are pleasures forevermore. (Psalm 16:9)

♦

Weeping may endure for a night, but joy cometh in the morning…Thou hast turned for me, my mourning into dancing … and girded me with gladness. (Psalm 30:5)

♦

Be glad in the Lord and rejoice, ye righteous: and shout for joy, all ye that are upright in heart. (Psalm 32:11)

♦

Our heart shall rejoice in Him, because we have trusted in his Holy Name. (Psalm 33:21)

♦

My soul shall be joyful in the Lord: it shall rejoice in His salvation. (Psalm 35:9)

♦

The righteous shall be glad in the Lord, and shall trust in Him; and all the upright in heart shall glory. (Psalm 64:10)

♦

They that sow in tears shall reap in joy. (Psalm 126:5)

◆

For as the heavens are higher than the earth, so are my ways higher than your ways, and my thoughts than your thoughts. For as the rain cometh down, and the snow from heaven, and returneth not thither, but watereth the earth, and maketh it bring forth and bud, that it may give seed to the sower, and bread to the eater:

So shall my word be that goeth forth out of my mouth: it shall not return unto me void, but it shall accomplish that which I please, and it shall prosper in the thing whereto I sent it. For ye shall go out with joy, and be led forth with peace: the mountains and the hills shall break forth before you into singing, and all the trees of the field shall clap their hands. (Isaiah 55:9-12)

◆

Ah Lord GOD! Behold, thou hast made the heaven and the earth by thy great power and stretched out arm, and there is nothing too hard for thee: Thou showest lovingkindness unto thousands, and recompensest the iniquity of the fathers into the bosom of their children after them:

the Great, the Mighty God, the LORD of hosts, is his name, Great in counsel, and mighty in work: for Thine eyes are open upon all the ways of the sons of men: to give every one according to his ways, and according to the fruit of his doings. (Jeremiah 32:17-19)

♦

The redeemed of the Lord shall return and come with singing unto Zion; and everlasting joy shall be upon their head: they shall obtain gladness and joy; and sorrow and mourning shall flee away. (Isaiah 51:11)

♦

I say unto you, that likewise joy shall be in heaven over one sinner that repenteth, more than over ninety and nine just persons, which need no repentance ... Likewise, I say unto you, there is joy in the presence of the angels of God over one sinner that repenteth. (Luke 15:7-10)

♦

These things have I spoken unto you, that my joy might remain in you, and that your joy might be full. (John 15:11)

◆

I will see you again, and your heart shall rejoice, and your joy, no man taketh from you. Hitherto have ye asked nothing in my name: ask and ye shall receive, that your joy may be full. These things I have spoken unto you, that in Me you might have peace. In the world ye shall have tribulation, but be of good cheer; I have overcome the world. (John 16:22-33)

◆

Thou hast made known to me the ways of life; thou shalt make me full of joy with thy countenance. (Acts 2:28)

◆

The kingdom of God is not meat and drink, but righteousness, and peace, and joy in the Holy Ghost. (Romans 14:17)

◆

Now the God of hope, fill you with all joy and peace in believing, that ye may abound in hope, through the power of the Holy Ghost. (Romans 15:13)

◆

The fruit of the Spirit is love,

joy, peace, patience, goodness, gentleness and self- control. (Galatians 5:22)

♦

Rejoice in the Lord always: Again I say rejoice. (Philippians 4:4)

♦

Whom having not seen, ye love; in whom, though now ye see Him not, yet believing, ye rejoice with joy unspeakable and full of glory. (1 Peter 1:8)

❧

SCRIPTURES ON CONTENTMENT

Rest in the Lord and wait patiently for Him: fret not thyself because of him who prospereth in his way…A little that a righteous man hath is better than the riches of many wicked. (Psalm 37:7)

♦

A merry heart maketh a cheerful countenance … He that is of a merry heart hath a continual feast … A merry heart doeth good like a medicine. (Proverbs 15:13)

♦

Do not be anxious about anything, but in everything, by prayer and petition, with thanksgiving, present your request to God, which transcends all understanding and will guard your hearts and minds in Christ Jesus. (Philippians 4:6-7)

♦

I have learned in whatsoever

state I am, therewith to be content. (Philippians 4:11)

♦

Godliness with contentment is great gain. (1 Timothy 6:6)

♦

For God did not give us a spirit of fear, but of power, love and a sound mind. (2 Timothy 1:7)

♦

Be content with such things as ye have; for He hath said, I never leave thee, nor forsake thee. (Hebrews 13:5)

♦

"Christianity alone teaches that our only way for reconciliation with God is by his grace that is received through faith."—Pastor Robert Jeffress, First Baptist Dallas

♦

"The attitude of the heart that causes faith to work is love, and love works in an atmosphere of humility."—Pastor Billy Joe Daugherty, Victory Christian Center, Tulsa, OK

❧

BELIEVE IN THE HOLY SPIRIT WITHIN YOU

Scriptures to believe in:

Jesus said "I tell you the truth. It is expedient for you that I go away: for if I go not away, the Comforter will not come unto you; but if I depart, I will send Him unto you ….

When the Spirit of truth is come, He will guide you into all truth: For He shall not speak of Himself; but whatsoever He shall hear, that will He speak; and He will show you things to come. He shall glorify Me; for He shall receive of mine and shall show it unto you. (John 16:7, 13-14)

♦

And he said unto them, I beheld Satan as lightning fall from heaven. Behold, I give unto you power to tread on serpents and scorpions, and over all the power of the enemy: and nothing shall by any means hurt you.

Notwithstanding in this rejoice not, that the spirits are subject unto you; but rather rejoice, because your names are written in heaven. In that hour Jesus rejoiced in spirit, and said, I thank thee, O Father, Lord of heaven and earth, that thou hast hid these things from the wise and prudent, and hast revealed them unto babes: even so, Father; for so it seemed good in thy sight.

All things are delivered to me of my Father: and no man knoweth who the Son is, but the Father; and who the Father is, but the Son, and he to whom the Son will reveal him. And he turned him unto his disciples, and said privately, Blessed are the eyes which see the things that ye see. (Luke 10:18-23)

♦

But ye shall receive power, after the Holy Ghost has come upon you. (Acts 1:8)

♦

If the Spirit of Him who raised up Christ from the dead dwell in you, he that raised up Christ shall also quicken your mortal bodies by his Spirit that dwelleth in you. (Romans 8:11)

♦

The Spirit also helpeth our infirmities: for we know not what we should pray for as we ought; but the Spirit itself maketh intercession for us.

(Romans 8:26)

♦

Now the God of hope fill you with all joy and peace in believing, that ye may abound in hope, through the power of the Holy Ghost. (Romans 15:13)

♦

God hath not given us the spirit of fear; but of power, and of love, and of a sound mind. That good thing that was committed unto thee, keep by the Holy Ghost which dwelleth in us. (2 Timothy1:7)

♦

The fruits of the Holy Spirit are love, joy, peace, patience, kindness, goodness, faithfulness, gentleness and self-control. (Galatians 5:22)

♦

Now unto him who is able to do immeasurably more than all we ask or imagine, according to his power that is at work within us, to Him be the glory in the church and in Christ Jesus throughout all generations forever and ever! Amen. (Ephesians 3:20)

♦

That the God of our Lord Jesus Christ, the Father of glory, may give unto you the spirit of wisdom and revelation in the knowledge of him:

The eyes of your understanding being enlightened; that ye may know what is the hope of his calling, and what the riches of the glory of his inheritance in the saints, And what is the exceeding greatness of his power to usward who believe, according to the working of his mighty power,

Which he wrought in Christ, when he raised him from the dead, and set him at his own right hand in the heavenly places, Far above all principality, and power, and might, and dominion, and every name that is named, not only in this world, but also in that which is to come:

And hath put all things under his feet, and gave him to be the head over all things to the church, Which is his body, the fullness of Him that filleth all in all. (Ephesians 1:17-23)

And it shall come to pass in the last days, saith God, I will pour out of my Spirit upon all flesh: and your sons and your daughters shall prophesy, and your young men shall see visions, and your old men shall dream dreams:

And on my servants and on my handmaidens I will pour out in those days of my Spirit; and they shall prophesy:

And I will shew wonders in heaven above, and signs in the earth beneath; blood, and fire, and vapor of smoke: The sun shall be turned into darkness, and the moon into blood, before that great and notable day of the Lord come:

And it shall come to pass, that whosoever shall call on the name of the Lord shall be saved. (Acts 2:17-21)

♦

But he, being full of the Holy Ghost, looked up steadfastly into heaven, and saw the glory of God, and Jesus standing on the right hand of God, and said, Behold, I see the heavens opened, and the Son of man standing on the right hand of God. Then they cried out with a loud voice, and stopped their ears, and ran upon him with one accord. (Acts 7:55-57)

♦

Wherefore I also, after I heard of your faith in the Lord Jesus, and love unto all the saints, Cease not to give thanks for you, making mention of you in my prayers;

That the God of our Lord Jesus Christ, the Father of glory, may give unto you the spirit of wisdom and revelation in the knowledge of him. (Ephesians 1:15-17)

♦

Pastor Donnie Swaggart of Family Worship Center, Baton Rouge, LA, stated:

The Holy Spirit brings life. Wherever the Holy Spirit is allowed to move, great things happen. The life of the Spirit ushers in new converts, heals the sick, breaks bondages, brings forth revelation, and glorifies Christ.

The Feast of Pentecost was the second greatest event in human history, with Calvary being the greatest. This event would do more to change the world for good than any other happening outside of Calvary. At this moment, the Holy Spirit came, the church was born, and the world has never been the same. Since that day, nearly 1 billion people all around the world have been filled with the Holy Spirit. Presently, at least a quarter of the world's 2 billion Christians embrace the Pentecostal message.

❧

BELIEVE FOR HEALTH AND WELL-BEING

Scriptures to believe in:

If you will hearken diligently to the voice of the Lord your God and will do what is right in His sight, and will listen to and obey all of His commandments, I will put none of these diseases upon you which I brought upon the Egyptians, for I am the Lord who heals you. (Exodus 15:26)

♦

You shall serve the Lord your God; He shall bless your bread and water and will take sickness from your midst. (Exodus 23:25)

♦

My son, attend to my words; Let them not depart from your sight; keep them in the center of your heart. For they are life to those who find them, healing and health to their flesh. Guard your heart with all diligence, for out of it flow the springs of life. (Proverbs 4:20-23)

♦

Bless the Lord, O my soul and forget not all of His benefits—Who forgives all of your iniquities, Who heals all of your diseases, Who redeems your life from the pit and corruption, and crowns you with loving-kindness and tender mercy; Who satisfies your mouth with good so that your youth renewed is like the eagle's. (Psalm 103:2-5)

♦

They cry to the Lord in their trouble, and He delivers them from their distresses. He sends His word and heals them and rescues them from the pit and destruction. Oh, that men would praise the Lord for His goodness and loving-kindness and His wonderful works to the children of men. (Psalm 107:19-21)

♦

I shall not die but live and declare the works of the Lord. (Psalm 118:7)

♦

Those who wait upon the Lord shall renew their strength. They will soar on wings like eagles; they will run and not grow weary, they will walk and not faint. (Isaiah 40:29)

♦

For I will restore health to you, and I will heal your wounds, says the Lord. (Jeremiah 30:17)

♦

Jesus fulfilled what was spoken by the prophet Isaiah, He Himself took our weaknesses and infirmities, and bore away our diseases. (Matthew 8:17)

♦

And if the Spirit of Him who raised Christ from the dead is living in you, He who raised Christ from the dead will also give life to your mortal bodies through his Spirit, who lives in you. (Romans 8:11)

♦

He himself bore our sins in His body, so that we might die to sin and live for righteousness; by His wounds you are healed. (1 Peter 2:24)

♦

Being confident of this, that He who began a good work in you will carry it on to completion until the day of Christ Jesus. (Philippians 1:6)

BELIEVE FOR YOUR FAMILY

Scriptures to believe in:

For I will pour water on him who is thirsty, and floods on the dry ground; I will pour My Spirit on your descendants, and My blessing on your offspring. (Isaiah 44:3)

♦

I will contend with him who contends with you and I will save your children. (Isaiah 49:25)

♦

All your children shall be taught by the Lord, and great shall be the peace of your children. (Isaiah 54:13)

♦

Train up a child in the way he should go, and when he is old he will not depart from it. (Proverbs 22:6)

♦

Correct your son and he will give you rest; yes, he will give delight to your soul. (Proverbs 29:17)

♦

He himself shall dwell in prosperity, and his descendants shall inherit the earth. (Psalm 25:13)

♦

I have been young, and now I am old; yet I have not seen the righteous forsaken, nor his descendants begging bread. (Psalm 37:25)

♦

He has blessed your children within you. (Psalm 147:13)

♦

Believe on the Lord Jesus Christ, and you will be saved, you and your household. (Acts 16:31)

♦

Therefore shall ye lay up these my words in your heart and in your soul, and bind them for a sign upon your hand, that they may be as frontlets between your eyes.

And ye shall teach them your children, speaking of them when thou sittest in thine house, and when thou walkest by the way, when thou liest down, and when thou risest up.

And thou shalt write them upon the door posts of thine house, and upon thy gates:

That your days may be multiplied, and the days of your children, in the land which the LORD sware unto your fathers to give them, as the days of heaven upon the earth.

For if ye shall diligently keep all these commandments which I command you, to do them, to love the LORD your God, to walk in all his ways, and to cleave unto him;

Then will the LORD drive out all these nations from before you, and ye shall possess greater nations and mightier than yourselves. (Deuteronomy 11:18-23)

♦

And God spoke all these words, saying, I am the LORD thy God, which have brought thee out of the land of Egypt, out of the house of bondage.

Thou shalt have no other gods before me. Thou shalt not make unto thee any graven image, or any likeness of anything that is in heaven above, or that is in the earth beneath, or that is in the water under the earth:

Thou shalt not bow down thyself to them, nor serve them: for I the LORD thy God am a jealous God, visiting the iniquity of the fathers upon the children unto the third and fourth generation of them that hate me; And shewing mercy unto thousands of them that love me, and keep my commandments.

Thou shalt not take the name of the LORD thy God in vain; for the LORD will not hold him guiltless that taketh His name in vain.

Remember the Sabbath day, to keep it holy. Six days shalt thou labor, and do all thy work: But the seventh day is the Sabbath of the LORD thy God: in it thou shalt not do any work, thou, nor thy son, nor thy daughter, thy manservant, nor thy maidservant, nor thy cattle, nor thy stranger that is within thy gates:

For in six days the LORD made heaven and earth, the sea, and all that in them is, and rested the seventh day: wherefore the LORD blessed the sabbath day, and hallowed it.

Honor thy father and thy mother: that thy days may be long upon the land which the LORD thy God giveth thee.

Thou shalt not commit adultery.

Thou shalt not steal.

Thou shalt not bear false witness against thy neighbor.

Thou shalt not covet thy neighbor's house, thou shalt not covet thy neighbor's wife, nor his manservant, nor his maidservant, nor his ox, nor his ass, nor any thing that is thy neighbor's.

And all the people saw the thundering, and the lightning, and the noise of the trumpet, and the mountain smoking. (Exodus.20:1-18)

♦

But the mercy of the LORD is from everlasting to everlasting upon them that fear him, and his righteousness unto children's children; To such as keep his covenant, and to those that remember his commandments to do them. The LORD hath prepared his throne in the heavens; and his kingdom ruleth over all. Bless the LORD, ye his angels, that excel in strength, that do his commandments, hearkening unto the voice of His word.

Bless ye the LORD, all ye his hosts; ye ministers of his, that do his pleasure. Bless the LORD, all his works in all places of his dominion: bless the LORD, O my soul. (Psalm 103:17-22)

♦

The LORD is high above all nations, and his glory above the heavens. Who is like unto the LORD our God, who dwelleth on high,

Who humbleth himself to behold the things that are in heaven, and in the earth! He raiseth up the poor out of the dust, and lifteth the needy out of the dunghill;

That he may set him with princes, even with the princes of his people. He maketh the barren woman to keep house, and to be a joyful mother of children. Praise ye the LORD. (Psalm 113:4-9)

QUOTATIONS ABOUT FAMILY

William Penn wrote August 4, 1682:

My dear Wife and Children: My love, which neither sea nor land nor death itself can extinguish or lessen toward you, most endearly visits you with eternal embraces, and will abide with you forever; and may the God of my life watch over you and bless you, and do good in this world and forever!

Some things are upon my spirit to leave with you in your respective capacities, as I am to the one a husband and to the rest a father, if I should never see you more in this world.

My dear wife, remember thou wast the love of my youth and much the joy of my life; the most beloved as well as the most worthy of all my earthly comforts; and the reason of that love was more thy inward than thy outward excellencies, which yet were many.

God knows, and thou knowest it, I can say it was a match of Providence's making and God's image in us both was the first thing, and the most amiable and engaging ornament in our eyes.

Now I am to leave thee, and that without knowing whether I shall ever see thee more in this world; take my counsel into thy bosom and let it dwell with thee in my stead while thou livest.

First: Let the fear of the Lord and a zeal and love to his glory dwell richly in thy heart; and thou wilt watch for good over thyself and thy dear children and family, that no rude, light, or bad thing be committed; else God will be offended, and He will repent Himself of the good He intends thee and thine ...

And now, my dearest, let me recommend to thy care my dear children; abundantly beloved of me as the Lord's blessings, and the sweet pledges of our mutual and endeared affection.

♦

Samuel Adams wrote to T. Wells, his daughter's fiancé, November 22, 1780:

> I could say a thousand things to you, if I had leisure. I could dwell on the importance of piety and religion, of industry and frugality, of prudence, economy, regularity and even Government, all of which are essential to the well-being of a family. But I have not time. I cannot however help repeating piety, because I think it indispensable. Religion in a family is at once its brightest ornament and its best security.

♦

Patrick Henry wrote in his Last Will and Testament, November 20, 1798:

> I have now disposed of all my property to my family; there is one thing more I wish I could give them, and that is the Christian religion. If they had that, and I had not given them one shilling, they would be rich, and if they had not that, and I had given them all the world, they would be poor. This is all the inheritance I give to my dear family. The religion of Christ will give them one which will make them rich indeed.

♦

Noah Webster wrote in *A Manual of Useful*

Studies, 1839, New Haven:

In the family are formed the elements of civil governments; the family discipline is the model of all social order ... the respect for the law and the magistrate begins in the respect for parents ...

Families are the nurseries of good and bad citizens. The parent who neglects to restrain and govern his child, or who, by his example, corrupts him, is the enemy of the community to which he belongs; the parent who instructs his child in good principles, and subjects him to correct discipline, is the guardian angel of his child, and the best benefactor of society.

Practical truths in religion, in morals, and in all civil and social concerns, ought to be among the first and most prominent objects of instruction. Without a competent knowledge of legal and social rights and duties, persons are often liable to suffer in property or reputation, by neglect or mistakes.

Without religious and moral principles deeply impressed on the mind, and controlling the whole conduct, science and literature will not make men what the laws of God require them to be; and without both kinds of knowledge, citizens can not enjoy the blessings which they seek.

♦

President Calvin Coolidge stated in New York, 1924:

The three fundamentals of scouthood are reverence for nature ... reverence for law ... and reverence for God. It is hard to see how a great man can be an atheist. Doubters do not achieve. No man realizes his full possibilities unless he has the deep conviction that life is eternally important, and that his work, well done, is part of an unending plan.

The first editions of the *Scout Handbook* (1911, 1915, 1927) explained of the 12th point of the Scout Law, "A Scout is Reverent":

He is reverent toward God. He is faithful in his religious duties and respects the convictions of others in matters of custom and religion.

The *Scout Handbook*–5th edition (1948) explained "Duty to God":

You worship God regularly with your family in your church or synagogue. You try to follow the religious teachings that you have been taught, and you are faithful in your church school duties, and help in church activities. Above all you are faithful to Almighty God's Commandments.

Most great men in history have been men of deep religious faith. Washington knelt in the snow to pray at Valley Forge. Lincoln always sought Divine guidance before each important decision. Be proud of your religious faith.

Remember in doing your duty to God, to be grateful to Him. Whenever you succeed in doing something well, thank Him for it. Sometimes when you look up into the starlit sky on a quiet night, and feel close to Him—thank Him as the Giver of all good things.

One way to express your duty and your thankfulness to God is to help others, and this too, is a part of your Scout promise.

♦

President Dwight Eisenhower stated in his message at the annual convention of the National Catholic Family Life Conference, New Orleans, March 25, 1954:

The destiny of the nation is as great in promise as its young people are great in character. In that light, we need constant and profound appreciation of the mother as a builder of a brighter and better future.

♦

President Dwight Eisenhower stated on June 14, 1954, as he signed into law Congressional Act, Joint Resolution 243 adding the phrase "one Nation under God" to the Pledge of Allegiance:

And this same study showed A deep reverence for the importance of family ties and religious belief. There is sin and evil in the world, and we're enjoined by Scripture and the Lord Jesus to oppose it with all our might.

♦

President Ronald Reagan wrote:

The family has always been the cornerstone of American society. Our families nurture, preserve, and pass on to each succeeding generation the values we share and cherish, values that are the foundation for our freedoms.

In the family we learn our first lessons of God and man, love and discipline, rights and responsibilities, human dignity and human frailty. Our families give us daily examples of these lessons being put into practice.

In raising and instructing our children, in providing personal and compassionate care for the elderly, in maintaining the spiritual strength of religious commitment among our people—in these and other ways, America's families make immeasurable contributions to America's well-being.

Today more than ever, it is essential that these contributions not be taken for granted and that each of us remember that the strength of our families is vital to the strength of our nation.

◆

President John F. Kennedy wrote:

I urge all citizens to make this Thanksgiving not merely a holiday from their labors, but rather a day of contemplation. I ask the head of each family to recount to his children the story of the first New England Thanksgiving, thus to impress upon future generations the heritage of this nation born in toil, in danger, in purpose, and in the conviction that right and justice and freedom can through man's efforts persevere and come to fruition with the blessing of God.

Let us observe this day with reverence and with prayer that will rekindle in us the will and show us the way not only to preserve our blessings, but also to extend them to the four corners of the Earth. Let us by our example, as well as by our material aid, assist all peoples of all nations who are striving to achieve a better life in freedom.

♦

Pope John Paul II addressed over 375,000 people from 70 different countries in a Mass celebrated at Cherry Creek State Park, Colorado, as a part of "World Youth Day," Sunday, August 15, 1993, with Vice-President Al Gore in attendance:

A "culture of death" seeks to impose itself on our desire to live, and live to the full ... In our own century, as at no other time in history, the "culture of death" has assumed a social and institutional form of legality to justify the most horrible crimes against humanity: genocide, "final solutions," "ethnic cleansings" and massive taking of lives of human beings even before they are born, or before they reach the natural point of death ...

In much of contemporary thinking, any reference to a 'law' guaranteed by the Creator is absent. There remains only each individual's choice of this or that objective as convenient or useful in a given set of circumstances. No longer is anything considered intrinsically 'good' and 'universally binding' ...

Vast sectors of society are confused about what is right and what is wrong and are at the mercy of those with the power to 'create' opinion and impose it on others ...

The family especially is under attack. And the sacred character of Human Life is denied. Naturally, the weakest members of society are the most at risk. The unborn, children, the sick, the handicapped, the old, the poor and unemployed, the immigrant and refugee ...

Do not be afraid to go out on the streets and into public places ... This is no time to be ashamed of the

Gospel. It is a time to preach it from the rooftops ...

You must feel the full urgency of the task. Woe to you if you do not succeed in defending life. The church needs your energies, your enthusiasm, your youthful ideas, in order to make the Gospel of Life penetrate the fabric of society, transforming people's hearts and the structures of society in order to create a civilization of true justice and love.

♦

Pope John Paul II stated in his farewell address from Stapleton International Airport, Denver, Colorado, August 15, 1993:

The "culture of life" means respect for nature and protection of God's work of creation ... In a special way, it means respect for Human Life from the first moment of conception until its natural end.

♦

Representative J.C. Watts, Jr., delivered the Republican response to President Clinton's State of the Union Address, February 5, 1997:

We believe first of all that the state of this union really isn't determined in Washington, D.C. It never has been, and it never will be. But for a long time the federal government has been grabbing too much power and too much authority over all of the people ...

The strength of America is not in Washington, the strength of America is at home in lives well lived in the land of faith and family. The strength of America is not on Wall Street but on Main Street, not in big business but in small business with local owners and workers. It's not in Congress, it's in the city hall. And I pray Republicans and Democrats both understand this ...

First, we can help our country by bringing back the knowledge, the ancient wisdom, that we're nothing without our spiritual, traditional and family values ... I didn't get my values from Washington. I got my values from my parents, from Buddy and Helen Watts, in Eufaula, Oklahoma.

I got my values growing up in a poor black neighborhood on the east side of the railroad tracks, where money was scarce but dreams were plentiful and love was all around. I got my values from a strong family, a strong church and a strong neighborhood.

I wasn't raised to be a Republican or Democrat. My parents just taught by example. They taught me and my brothers and sisters that, if you lived under their roof, you were going to work.

They taught us, if you made a mistake, as we all do, you've got to own up to it, you call it what it is, and you try to turn it around. They taught us, if you spend more money than you make, you're on a sure road to disaster.

I was taught to respect everyone for the simple reason that we're all God's children. I was taught, in the words of Dr. Martin Luther King, Jr., and from my uncle, Wade Watts, to judge a man not by the color of his skin, but by the content of his character. And I was taught that character does count, and that character is simply doing what's right when nobody's looking.

❧

BELIEVE GOD'S PROMISES FOR PROTECTION

Scriptures to believe in:

Because you have made the Lord, who is my refuge, even the Most High, your dwelling place, no evil shall befall you, nor shall any plague come near your dwelling. For He has given His angels charge over you, to keep you in all your ways. In their hands they shall bear you up, lest you dash your foot against a stone. (Psalm 91:9-12)

(Thank the Lord for giving charge to His angels to protect you and your loved ones every day!)

♦

The angel of the Lord encamps all around those who fear Him, and delivers them. (Psalm 34:7)

♦

I will lift up mine eyes unto the hills, from whence cometh my help. My help cometh from the LORD, which made heaven and earth. He will not suffer thy foot to be moved: he that keepeth thee will not slumber. Behold, he that keepeth Israel shall neither slumber nor sleep.

The LORD is thy keeper: the LORD is thy shade upon thy right hand. The sun shall not smite thee by day, nor the moon by night. The LORD shall preserve thee from all evil: he shall preserve thy soul. The Lord shall preserve thy going out and thy coming in from this time forth, and even for evermore. (Psalm.121:1-8)

♦

A bruised reed, He shall not break, and the smoking flax shall He not quench: He shall bring forth judgment unto truth. He shall not fail nor be discouraged, till He has set judgment in the earth: and the isles shall wait for his law.

Thus saith God the LORD, He that created the heavens, and stretched them out; He that spread forth the earth, and that which cometh out of it; He that giveth breath unto the people upon it, and spirit to them that walk therein: I the LORD have called thee in righteousness, and will hold thine hand, and will keep thee, and give thee for a covenant of the people, for a light of the Gentiles; To open the blind eyes, to bring out the prisoners from the prison, and them that sit in darkness out of the dungeon. (Isaiah.42:3-7)

♦

Sharon Daugherty wrote in *Praise and Worship-A Key to Victory,* 2020:

Because we live in a fallen world and there is an enemy who oppresses us, there are times when our faith in God will be challenged. We have to determine ahead of time to have a fixed heart upon God's Word.

We are living in what the Bible refers to as the last days, and the enemy has intensified his efforts to stop God's Kingdom from advancing before his time is up and he is removed from the Earth. Psalm 108:1 says "O God, my heart is fixed; I will sing and give praise ..."

The Modern English Version of this verse says, "O God, my heart is determined; I will sing and give praise with my whole heart."

∽

QUOTATIONS ABOUT BELIEVING GOD FOR PROTECTION

Rev. Henry Muhlenberg, whose one son, Frederick, was the first Speaker of the U.S. House of Representatives, and another son, John Peter, was a General in the Revolution and a U.S. Congressman, stated:

> From all appearances General Washington does not belong to the so-called world of society, for he respects God's Word, believes in the atonement through Christ, and bears himself in humility and gentleness. Therefore, the Lord God has also singularly, yea, marvelously preserved him from harm in the midst of countless perils, ambuscades, fatigues, etc., and has hitherto graciously held him in his hand as a chosen vessel.

♦

President Grover Cleveland issued a Proclamation of a National Day of Thanksgiving and Prayer, October 25, 1887:

The goodness and the mercy of God, which have followed the American people during all the days of the past year, claim their grateful recognition and humble acknowledgment.

By His omnipotent power He has protected us from war and pestilence and from every national calamity; by His gracious favor the earth has yielded a generous return to the labor of the husbandman, and every path of honest toil has led to comfort and contentment;

By His loving kindness the hearts of our people have been replenished with fraternal sentiment and patriotic endeavor, and by His unerring guidance we have been directed in the way of national prosperity.

❦

BELIEVE FOR THE FUTURE OF OUR NATION

Pastor Jack Hibbs of Calvary Chapel Chino Hills wrote:

> We see it repeatedly throughout the Bible in examples such as Nehemiah, Josiah, and Hezekiah. First, these men personally renewed themselves in the Lord, and then they set out to influence their culture and their nation for what was right.
>
> It started with just one individual unabashedly willing to turn back to God, and soon an entire generation of God's people did the same. Only after these leaders began to seek the ways of the Lord was there a profound cultural shift.
>
> It happened as well in America's great awakenings. In each case, there was a ripple effect. A radical awakening, a change, repentance, that took place in God's people, bringing about a dramatic shift to

the culture at large. The result was a witness to the lost, which brought salvation to many.

♦

Dr. D. James Kennedy of Coral Ridge Ministries stated:

> How much more forcefully can I say it? The time has come, and it is long overdue, when Christians and conservatives and all men and women who believe in the birthright of freedom must rise up and reclaim America for Jesus Christ.

♦

Pastor Rob McCoy of Godspeak Calvary Chapel, Thousand Oaks, CA, stated:

> Landing at an unintended destination blown far of course from where they were to be, exhausted but in God's Providence, they were not lost.
>
> Though revisionist history would seek to erase the countless miracles that would sustain and establish them in this land, the truth is, they not only survived but flourished and established a foothold in this new land that would be the beginning of freedom the world had yet to know.

Now, 400 years later their conception of freedom has established a land where all the world comes to be free. In this season of strife and fear, that has caused mankind the world over to surrender their freedom for the deception of safety which in reality has reduced the torch of freedom to a flickering candle, we today must look back and remember the Pilgrim's bravery and resolve to place such a high value on the celestial article of freedom.

They risked everything and so must we. They had no examples to follow when they ventured far from comfort in quest of freedom. We today simply need to look back and see this has been done before and must be done now.

May we as Americans awaken to our rich heritage and once again stand in defiance of tyranny for the freedom of man.

❧

BELIEVE GOD'S PROMISE OF ETERNAL LIFE IN HEAVEN

Scriptures to believe in:

Whom have I in heaven but thee? and there is none upon earth that I desire beside thee. My flesh and my heart faileth: but God is the strength of my heart, and my portion forever.

For, lo, they that are far from thee shall perish: thou hast destroyed all them that go a whoring from thee. But it is good for me to draw near to God: I have put my trust in the Lord GOD, that I may declare all thy works. (Psalm 73:25-28)

◆

For the word of the LORD is right; and all his works are done in truth. He loveth righteousness and judgment: the earth is full of the goodness of the LORD.

By the word of the LORD were the heavens made; and all the host of them by the breath of his mouth.

He gathereth the waters of the sea together as an heap: he layeth up the depth in storehouses. Let all the earth fear the LORD: let all the inhabitants of the world stand in awe of him. (Psalm 33:4-8)

♦

Thy mercy, O LORD, is in the heavens; and thy faithfulness reacheth unto the clouds. Thy righteousness is like the great mountains; thy judgments are a great deep: O LORD, thou preservest man and beast. How excellent is thy lovingkindness, O God! therefore the children of men put their trust under the shadow of Thy wings. (Psalm 36:5-7)

♦

And seeing the multitudes, he went up into a mountain: and when he was set, his disciples came unto him: And he opened his mouth, and taught them, saying,

Blessed are the poor in spirit: for theirs is the kingdom of heaven.

Blessed are they that mourn: for they shall be comforted.

Blessed are the meek: for they shall inherit the earth.

Blessed are they which do hunger and thirst after righteousness: for they shall be filled.

Blessed are the merciful: for they shall obtain mercy.

Blessed are the pure in heart: for they shall see God.

Blessed are the peacemakers: for they shall be called the children of God.

Blessed are they which are persecuted for righteousness' sake: for theirs is the kingdom of heaven.

Blessed are ye, when men shall revile you, and persecute you, and shall say all manner of evil against you falsely, for my sake.

Rejoice, and be exceeding glad: for great is your reward in heaven: for so persecuted they the prophets which were before you.

Ye are the salt of the earth: but if the salt have lost his savour, wherewith shall it be salted? it is thenceforth good for nothing, but to be cast out, and to be trodden under foot of men. Ye are the light of the world. A city that is set on a hill cannot be hid. (Matthew 5:1-14)

◆

But I say unto you, Love your enemies, bless them that curse you, do good to them that hate you, and pray for them which despitefully use you, and persecute you; That ye may be the children of your Father which is in heaven: for he maketh his sun to rise on the evil and on the good, and sendeth rain on the just and on the unjust. For if ye love them which love you, what reward have ye?

Do not even the publicans the same? And if ye salute your brethren only, what do ye more than others? Do not even the publicans so? Be ye therefore perfect, even as your Father which is in heaven is perfect. (Matthew 5:44-48)

◆

After this manner therefore pray ye: Our Father which art in heaven, Hallowed be thy name. Thy kingdom come. Thy will be done in earth, as it is in heaven. Give us this day our daily bread. And forgive us our debts, as we forgive our debtors. And lead us not into temptation, but deliver us from evil:

For thine is the kingdom, and

the power, and the glory forever and ever. (Matthew 6:9-13)

♦

Another parable put he forth unto them, saying, The kingdom of heaven is like to a grain of mustard seed, which a man took, and sowed in his field: Which indeed is the least of all seeds: but when it is grown, it is the greatest among herbs, and becometh a tree, so that the birds of the air come and lodge in the branches thereof.

Another parable spake he unto them; The kingdom of heaven is like unto leaven, which a woman took, and hid in three measures of meal, till the whole was leavened.

All these things spake Jesus unto the multitude in parables; and without a parable spake he not unto them: That it might be fulfilled which was spoken by the prophet, saying, I will open my mouth in parables; I will utter things which have been kept secret from the foundation of the world. (Matthew 13:31-35)

♦

And then if any man shall say to you, Lo, here is Christ; or, lo, he is there; believe him not: For false christs and false prophets shall rise, and shall shew signs and wonders, to seduce, if it were possible, even the elect.

But take ye heed: behold, I have foretold you all things. But in those days, after that tribulation, the sun shall be darkened, and the moon shall not give her light, And the stars of heaven shall fall, and the powers that are in heaven shall be shaken. And then shall they see the Son of man coming in the clouds with great power and glory. And then shall he send his angels, and shall gather together his elect from the four winds, from the uttermost part of the earth to the uttermost part of heaven.

So ye in like manner, when ye shall see these things come to pass, know that it is nigh, even at the doors. Verily I say unto you, that this generation shall not pass, till all these things be done. Heaven and earth shall pass away: but my words shall not pass away. But of that day and that hour knoweth no man, no, not the angels which are in heaven, neither the Son, but the Father.

Take ye heed, watch and pray: for ye know not when the time is. For the Son of man is as a man taking a far journey, who left his house, and gave authority to his servants, and to every man his work, and commanded the porter to watch. Watch ye therefore: for ye know not when the master of the house cometh, at even, or at midnight, or at the cockcrowing, or in the morning. (Mark 13:21-35)

♦

They said therefore unto him, What sign shewest thou then, that we may see, and believe thee? Our fathers did eat manna in the desert; as it is written, He gave them bread from heaven to eat.

Then Jesus said unto them, Verily, verily, I say unto you, Moses gave you not that bread from heaven; but my Father giveth you the true bread from heaven. For the bread of God is he which cometh down from heaven, and giveth life unto the world.

Then said they unto him, Lord, evermore give us this bread. And Jesus said unto them, I am the bread of life: he that cometh to me shall never hunger; and he that believeth on me shall never thirst.

But I said unto you, That ye also have seen me, and believe not. All that the Father giveth me shall come to me; and him that cometh to me I will in no wise cast out. For I came down from heaven, not to do mine own will, but the will of him that sent me. (John 6:30-38)

♦

Father, glorify thy name. Then came there a voice from heaven, saying, I have both glorified it, and will glorify it again. The people therefore, that stood by, and heard it, said that it thundered: others said, An angel spake to him. Jesus answered and said, This voice came not because of me, but for your sakes. Now is the judgment of this world: now shall the prince of this world be cast out. And I, if I be lifted up from the earth, will draw all men unto me. (John12:28-32)

♦

Immediately after the tribulation of those days shall the sun be darkened, and the moon shall not give her light, and the stars shall fall from heaven, and the powers of the heavens shall be shaken:

And then shall appear the sign of the Son of man in heaven: and then shall all the tribes of the earth mourn, and they shall see the Son of man coming in the clouds of heaven with power and great glory. And he shall send his angels with a great sound of a trumpet, and they shall gather together his elect from the four winds, from one end of heaven to the other. (Matthew 24:29-31)

♦

And he said unto them, Go ye into all the world, and preach the gospel to every creature. He that believeth and is baptized shall be saved; but he that believeth not shall be damned. And these signs shall follow them that believe; In my name shall they cast out devils; they shall speak with new tongues; They shall take up serpents; and if they drink any deadly thing, it shall not hurt them; they shall lay hands on the sick, and they shall recover.

So then after the Lord had spoken unto them, he was received up into heaven, and sat on the right hand of God. And they went forth, and preached everywhere, the Lord working with them, and confirming

the word with signs following. Amen.
(Mark 16:15-20)

♦

And Jesus came and spake unto
them, saying, All power is given unto
me in heaven and in earth.

Go ye therefore, and teach all
nations, baptizing them in the name
of the Father, and of the Son, and of
the Holy Ghost: Teaching them to
observe all things whatsoever I have
commanded you: and, lo, I am with
you always, even unto the end of the
world. Amen. (Matthew 28:18-20)

♦

But God, who is rich in mercy,
for his great love wherewith he loved
us, Even when we were dead in sins,
hath quickened us together with
Christ, (by grace ye are saved;) And
hath raised us up together, and made
us sit together in heavenly places in
Christ Jesus: That in the ages to come
he might shew the exceeding riches
of His grace in his kindness toward
us through Christ Jesus.

For by grace are ye saved through
faith; and that not of yourselves: it is
the gift of God: Not of works, lest
any man should boast. For we are his

workmanship, created in Christ Jesus unto good works, which God hath before ordained that we should walk in them. (Ephesians 2:4-10)

♦

Wherefore God also hath highly exalted him, and given him a name which is above every name: That at the name of Jesus every knee should bow, of things in heaven, and things in earth, and things under the earth; And that every tongue should confess that Jesus Christ is Lord, to the glory of God the Father.

Wherefore, my beloved, as ye have always obeyed, not as in my presence only, but now much more in my absence, work out your own salvation with fear and trembling. For it is God which worketh in you both to will and to do of his good pleasure. Do all things without murmurings and disputings:

That ye may be blameless and harmless, the sons of God, without rebuke, in the midst of a crooked and perverse nation, among whom ye shine as lights in the world; Holding forth the word of life; that I may rejoice in the day of Christ, that I have not run in vain, neither laboured in vain. (Philippians 2:9-16)

But the righteousness which is of faith speaketh on this wise, Say not in thine heart, Who shall ascend into heaven? (that is, to bring Christ down from above:)

Or, Who shall descend into the deep? (that is, to bring up Christ again from the dead.) But what saith it? The word is nigh thee, even in thy mouth, and in thy heart: that is, the word of faith, which we preach;

That if thou shalt confess with thy mouth the Lord Jesus, and shalt believe in thine heart that God hath raised him from the dead, thou shalt be saved.

For with the heart man believeth unto righteousness; and with the mouth confession is made unto salvation.

For the scripture saith, Whosoever believeth on him shall not be ashamed. (Romans 10:6-11)

Blessed be the God and Father of our Lord Jesus Christ, which according to his abundant mercy hath begotten us again unto a lively hope by the resurrection of Jesus Christ from the dead,

To an inheritance incorruptible, and undefiled, and that fadeth not away, reserved in heaven for you, Who are kept by the power of God through faith unto salvation ready to be revealed in the last time. Wherein ye greatly rejoice. (1 Peter 1:3-6)

♦

For the Lord Himself shall descend from heaven with a shout, with the voice of the archangel, and with the trump of God: and the dead in Christ shall rise first: Then we which are alive and remain shall be caught up together with them in the clouds, to meet the Lord in the air: and so shall we ever be with the Lord. Wherefore comfort one another with these words. 1 (Thessalonians 4:16-18)

♦

And I heard a great voice out of heaven saying, Behold, the tabernacle of God is with men, and He will dwell with them, and they shall be his people, and God himself shall be with them, and be their God.

And God shall wipe away all tears from their eyes; and there shall be no more death, neither sorrow, nor crying, neither shall there be any more pain: for the former things are passed away.

And he that sat upon the throne said, Behold, I make all things new. And he said unto me, Write: for these words are true and faithful. And he said unto me, It is done. I am Alpha and Omega, the beginning and the end. I will give unto him that is athirst of the fountain of the water of life freely. He that overcometh shall inherit all things; and I will be his God, and he shall be my son. (Revelations 21:3-7)

♦

And I beheld, and I heard the voice of many angels round about the throne and the beasts and the elders: and the number of them was ten thousand times ten thousand, and thousands of thousands; Saying with a loud voice, Worthy is the Lamb that was slain to receive power, and riches, and wisdom, and strength, and honor, and glory, and blessing.

And every creature which is in

heaven, and on the earth, and under the earth, and such as are in the sea, and all that are in them, heard I saying, Blessing, and honor, and glory, and power, be unto him that sitteth upon the throne, and unto the Lamb for ever and ever. (Revelations 5:11-13)

Printed in the USA
CPSIA information can be obtained
at www.ICGtesting.com
JSHW010051050823
45878JS00002B/7

9 781736 959008